# HOUGHTON MIFFLIN HARCOURT

# JOURNEYS

## Program Authors

James F. Baumann · David J. Chard · Jamal Cooks
J. David Cooper · Russell Gersten · Marjorie Lipson
Lesley Mandel Morrow · John J. Pikulski · Héctor H. Rivera
Mabel Rivera · Shane Templeton · Sheila W. Valencia
Catherine Valentino · MaryEllen Vogt

## Consulting Author

Irene Fountas

Cover illustration by Valeria Docampo.

Printed in the U.S.A.

ISBN 10:    0-54-725191-2
ISBN 13:    978-0-54-725191-2

6789 - 0914 - 18 17 16 15 14 13 12
4500353302

# HOUGHTON MIFFLIN HARCOURT
## School Publishers

# Neighborhood Visit

**Big Idea** There are different kinds of communities.

# Nature Watch

**Big Idea** Nature can teach us many things.

# Unit 3

## Tell Me About It

**Big Idea** We learn from each other.

# Welcome, Reader!

You are about to begin a journey into reading. Along the way you will meet many new characters, such as a superhero dog. You'll also travel to the world of outer space and other exciting places. Your journey is sure to be filled with surprises, and you'll learn to be a better reader, too!

Get ready to meet some new friends with the story *Henry and Mudge*. Turn the page and let the fun begin!

Sincerely,

The Authors

# Neighborhood Visit

Unit 1

# Big Idea

There are different kinds of communities.

# Paired Selections

### TARGET VOCABULARY

**curly**

**straight**

**floppy**

**drooled**

**weighed**

**stood**

**collars**

**row**

Vocabulary Reader

Context Cards

# Vocabulary in Context

● Read each **Context Card**.

● Use a Vocabulary word to tell about something you did.

**1**
## curly
A poodle is a dog that has very curly hair.

**2**
## straight
Some kinds of dogs have long, straight hair.

### 3 floppy

Hound dogs have floppy ears. The ears hang down very low.

### 4 drooled

The Saint Bernard drooled all over the place!

### 5 weighed

A dog can be weighed on a scale. Then the vet knows how heavy the dog is.

### 6 stood

The dog stood still while it was measured.

### 7 collars

Collars come in different styles. A collar goes around a dog's neck.

### 8 row

The dog treats are lined up in a row on the shelf.

# Background

✔ **TARGET VOCABULARY** **At the Animal Shelter** If you want to adopt a dog, start at an animal shelter. A shelter may have a row of dogs to choose from. Some have dogs with curly fur or pointed ears. Shelters have even had dogs that stood three feet tall! Play with a few dogs before you choose one. Just be careful not to get drooled on! After you get a new dog, take it to a vet for an exam and to be weighed.

floppy ears

straight fur

collars

# Comprehension

✔ **TARGET SKILL** **Sequence of Events**

In *Henry and Mudge,* one event happens, and then
another and another. They follow in an order, or
sequence, of events. Use a chart like the one below to
show the sequence of the story events as you read.

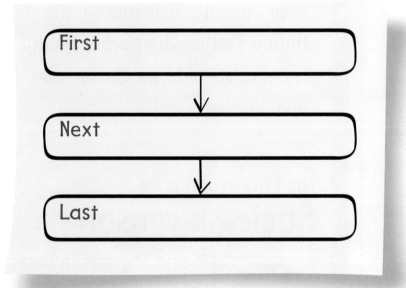

✔ **TARGET STRATEGY** **Infer/Predict**

Think about the sequence of story events and use what
you already know. Make predictions about the story as
you read *Henry and Mudge.* Then check to see if your
predictions are correct.

## TARGET VOCABULARY

| | |
|---|---|
| drooled | floppy |
| collars | stood |
| curly | straight |
| weighed | row |

## TARGET SKILL

**Sequence of Events**
Tell the order in which
things happen.

## TARGET STRATEGY

**Infer/Predict** Use
clues to figure out more
about story parts.

### GENRE
**Realistic fiction** is a
story that could happen
in real life.

## MEET THE AUTHOR
# Cynthia Rylant

Henry and Mudge have
starred in more than
twenty-five books
by Cynthia Rylant.
A musical based on
their adventures is touring the
United States. The part of Mudge
is being played by a grown man
in a dog costume!

## MEET THE ILLUSTRATOR
# Suçie Stevenson

Suçie Stevenson loves
drawing the character
of Mudge. In fact, she
has two big dogs of her
own. "They don't drool
as much as Mudge," she says.

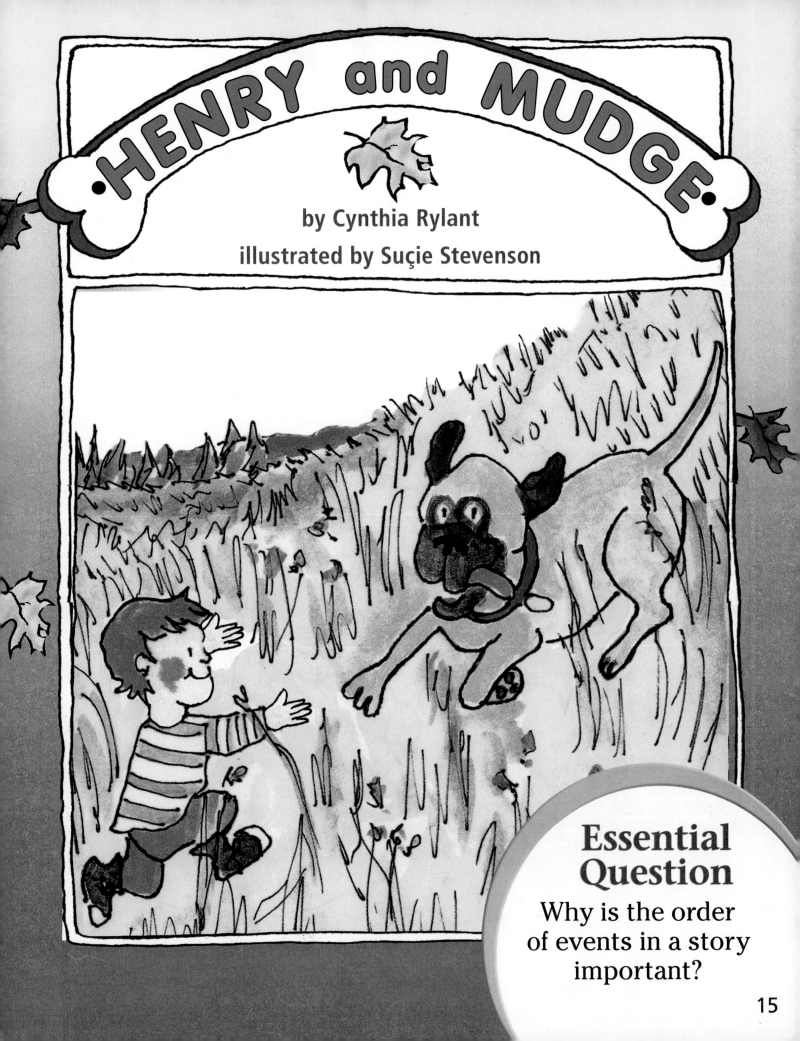

# HENRY and MUDGE

by Cynthia Rylant

illustrated by Suçie Stevenson

## Essential Question

Why is the order of events in a story important?

Henry had no brothers and no sisters.
"I want a brother," he told his parents.
"Sorry," they said.
Henry had no friends on his street.

"I want to live on a different street,"
he told his parents.

"Sorry," they said.

Henry had no pets at home.

"I want to have a dog," he told his parents.

"Sorry," they *almost* said.

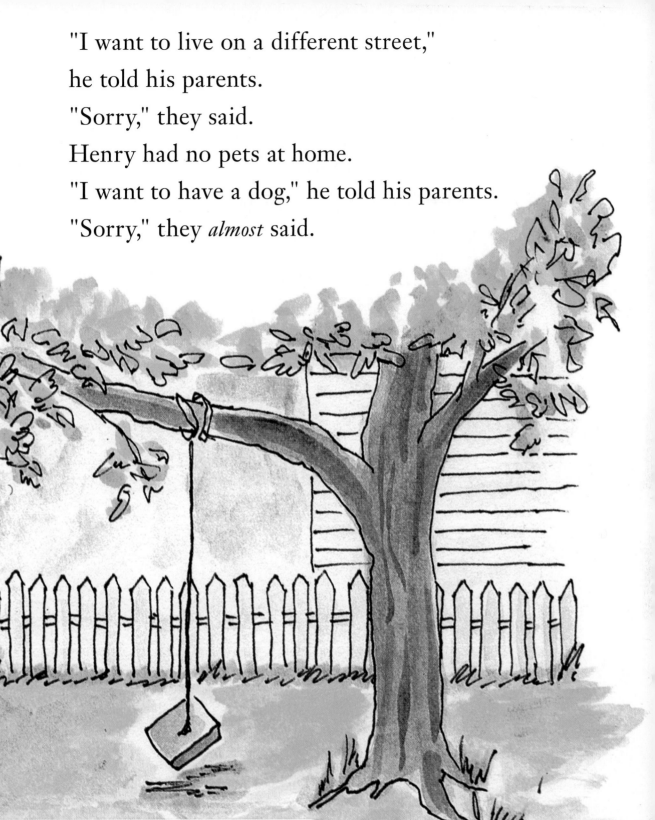

**STOP AND THINK**
**Infer/Predict** What might Henry's parents
say about getting a dog?
Check your prediction as you read.

But first they looked at their house
with no brothers and sisters.
Then they looked at their street
with no children.
Then they looked at Henry's face.

Then they looked at each other.
"Okay," they said.
"I want to hug you!" Henry told
his parents.
And he did.

✔️ STOP AND THINK
**Sequence of Events** What happened after Henry's parents looked at each other?

Henry searched for a dog.

"Not just any dog," said Henry.

"Not a short one," he said.

"Not a curly one," he said.

"And no pointed ears."

Then he found Mudge.

Mudge had floppy ears, not pointed.

And Mudge had straight fur, not curly.

But Mudge was short.

"Because he's a puppy," Henry said.

"He'll grow."

**STOP AND THINK**
**Author's Craft** What words does the author use to describe Mudge?

And did he ever!

He grew out of his puppy cage.

He grew out of his dog cage.

He grew out of seven collars in a row.

And when he finally stopped growing . . .

he weighed
one hundred eighty pounds,
he stood three feet tall,
and he drooled.
"I'm glad you're not short,"
Henry said.
And Mudge licked him,
then sat on him.

## How Pets Grow

**Write to Explain**

Mudge grew from a small puppy into a huge dog. Choose an animal, such as a dog, a cat, or a bird. Think about how the animal grows from a baby to an adult. Write two or three sentences that tell how the animal grows. Draw pictures to show your ideas. SCIENCE

## Turn and Talk — Events in Order

With a partner, look back through *Henry and Mudge.* Take turns telling each other what happens first, next, and last. How does knowing the order of events help you understand the story? SEQUENCE OF EVENTS

# All in the Family

by Katherine Mackin

At the San Antonio Zoo, you can see
many amazing animals. Some of these
animals may have a family member
living in your neighborhood!

# Different Kinds of **Dogs**

Bush dogs live in Central America and South America. They have straight, brown fur. In the wild, they eat large rodents.

Pet dogs come in all shapes and sizes. They may have floppy ears or curly hair. They eat food made for dogs. Pet dogs should wear collars.

# **Cats** of All Sizes

Lions belong to the cat family. They can grow up to eight feet long. Some have stood four feet tall. Lions hunt big animals in the wild.

Most house cats do not weigh more than fifteen pounds. They mostly eat special food for cats. However, some cats like to hunt for mice or birds.

## Large Lizards

Komodo dragons are the largest lizards. They can grow to ten feet long. Some have weighed five hundred pounds! The saliva of a Komodo dragon is dangerous. You would not want to be drooled on by a Komodo dragon!

## Little Lizards

Geckos belong to the lizard family. They are about eight inches long. Adult geckos weigh about one to two ounces. Geckos eat insects. They can eat ten crickets in a row.

# Making Connections

## Text to Self

**Make a List** Henry convinces his parents to get a dog.  What reasons does he give?  Imagine you want a new pet.  List your reasons.

## Text to Text

**Compare and Contrast** With a partner, pick one of the animals from "All in the Family."  Discuss how that animal is like and different from Mudge.  Ask questions if you don't understand something your partner says.

## Text to World

**Connect to Science** Choose an animal from "All in the Family" to research.  Make a list of questions and find the answers.  Then share the answers with a partner.

# Grammar

**Subjects and Predicates** The **subject** of
a sentence is the naming part. It tells
who or what did or does something.

Pam walks her dog.
The boy chooses a pet.

The **predicate** part of a sentence is the action part. It tells
what the subject did or does.

The dogs pull on a rope.
Ben plays with his dog.

 **Write each sentence. Then circle
the subject.**

❶ Mel grew tall.

❷ My father hugs the dog.

**Write each sentence. Draw a line under
the predicate.**

❶ The boys play ball.

❷ Susan fed her dog.

**Sentence Fluency** When two short sentences have the same predicate, you can put the sentences together. Join them to make one longer sentence. Write *and* between the two subjects. This will make your writing smoother.

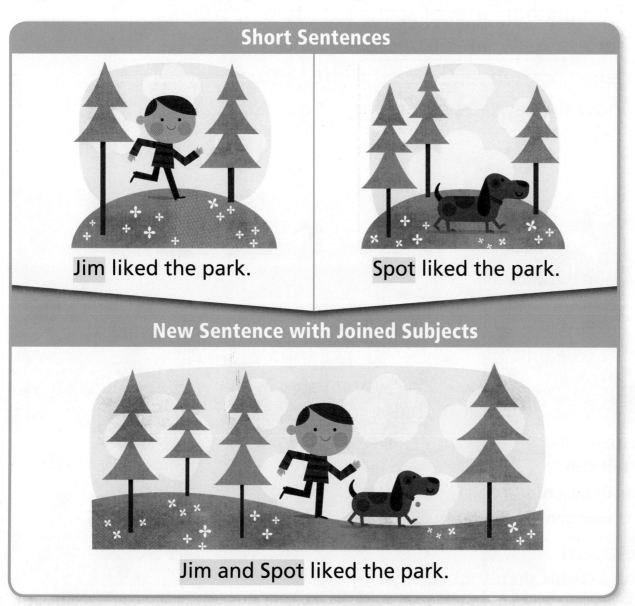

**Short Sentences**

Jim liked the park.

Spot liked the park.

**New Sentence with Joined Subjects**

Jim and Spot liked the park.

## Connect Grammar to Writing

**When you revise your sentences, try joining sentences that have the same predicate.**

# Write to Narrate

Use details when you write a **true story** about something that happened. Details help your reader picture what you are telling about.

Megan drafted some sentences for a true story. See how she revised her writing to add details.

## Writing Traits Checklist

✔ **Ideas**
Did I use details to tell the reader more?

✔ **Organization**
Did I tell about events in an order that makes sense?

✔ **Word Choice**
Did I use words that describe?

✔ **Voice**
Does my writing sound like the way I would tell the story?

## Revised Draft

My friend Lucy gave me a **beautiful** ^ bracelet with many colorful beads. She made it. She ^ calls it a friendship bracelet.

When I wear it I think of my best friend Lucy.

I love my ^ bracelet!

# A Gift

by Megan Stiles

My friend Lucy gave me a beautiful bracelet. She made it with many colorful beads. She calls it a friendship bracelet. When I wear it I think of my best friend Lucy. I love my bracelet!

I added details to my final paper to make it more interesting.

## Reading as a Writer

How do the words that Megan added help you picture what she is telling about? Where can you add details to your true story?

33

**TARGET VOCABULARY**

**remembered**

**porch**

**crown**

**spend**

**stuck**

**visit**

**cousin**

**piano**

Vocabulary
Reader

Context
Cards

# Vocabulary in Context

- Read each **Context Card**.

- Place the Vocabulary words in alphabetical order.

**1**   **remembered**

Mom remembered my birthday. She never forgets.

**2**   **porch**

They sat outside and talked on the front porch.

### 3 crown

This girl wears a crown on her head for her birthday.

### 4 spend

These girls spend time together. They play every day.

### 5 stuck

While on vacation, their car got stuck in the mud. It can't move.

### 6 visit

These grandparents like to visit. They see their grandchildren a lot.

### 7 cousin

My aunt and uncle have three children. Each child is my cousin.

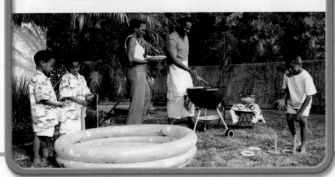

### 8 piano

The father teaches his child to play the piano, a musical instrument.

# Background

✔ **TARGET VOCABULARY** **Family Visits** What happens when families visit? Some families spend time sitting on a porch. Other families meet around a piano and sing songs. If someone gets stuck on the words, others help out. Many families gather for birthdays. The birthday boy or girl might wear a crown for the special day. No matter what a family does, the visit will be remembered for a long time!

grandfather

uncle

grandmother

cousin

aunt

mother

sister

father

me

# Comprehension

✔ **TARGET SKILL** **Compare and Contrast**

In *My Family,* you will find out how people in Camila's family are alike and different. As you read, use a Venn diagram like this one to compare and contrast details about Camila's family with your own family.

✔ **TARGET STRATEGY** **Question**

As you read, use your diagram to ask questions about how Camila's family members are alike and different. Questioning helps you understand what you read.

mi familia
my family

✔ **TARGET VOCABULARY**

| | |
|---|---|
| remembered | porch |
| crown | spend |
| stuck | visit |
| cousin | piano |

✔ **TARGET SKILL**

**Compare and Contrast** Tell how two things are alike or not.

✔ **TARGET STRATEGY**

**Question** Ask questions about what you are reading.

**GENRE**

**Informational text** gives facts about a topic.

**MEET THE AUTHOR AND PHOTOGRAPHER**

# George Ancona

George Ancona is often asked if he keeps in touch with the people he photographs. The answer is yes! Not long ago, he heard from the father of the young boy he had photographed for *Pablo Remembers*. Pablo, now grown, was getting married. Mr. Ancona went back to Mexico for the wedding.

# My Family

by George Ancona

## Essential Question

How are families alike and different?

I am Camila. I live in Miami with my
mother, Damaris, my father, Roberto, and my
brother, René. My mother came from Cuba.
My father came from Puerto Rico.

My mother and I go to school together.
That's because she teaches Spanish in my
school.  When we are at home, I like to help
her cook dinner.

Sometimes when my Grandma Marta comes
to visit, I dress up and put on a show for her.
Today she is teaching me a song. It goes like this:

*There once was a sailor at sea*
*who liked to play the guitar.*
*When he remembered his far away land*
*he picked his guitar, and started to sing:*
*On the high sea, on the high sea, on the*
*high sea. [repeat]*

René is my little brother. Our friends and
family come to the house for his birthday. We play
games, eat, and sing "Happy Birthday" to him.

**STOP AND THINK**
**Question** What questions might you ask René about his birthday party?

Here is my family: Grandmother Marta and
Grandfather Rigoberto had four children. Almost
all of them came to René's birthday party.

Marta & Rigoberto

| Andrés & Darleen | María Irene & Victor | Martica & Miguel | Damaris & Roberto | ◀ They married: |
|---|---|---|---|---|
| Victor Mar Isabel | Victoria Valeria Vanesa | Gabriela Leticia | René Camila | And they had these ◀ children: |

Grandma came with Aunt María Irene and
Victoria. Uncle Andrés came with Victor and Mar
Isabel. Aunt Martica, Uncle Miguel, Gabriela, and
Leticia came too. Soon the house was full.

We played many games.
Aunt María Irene showed us
how to play hopscotch.  Little
Leticia put on a crown to dance.
Grandpa Rigoberto danced with
cousin Mar Isabel.

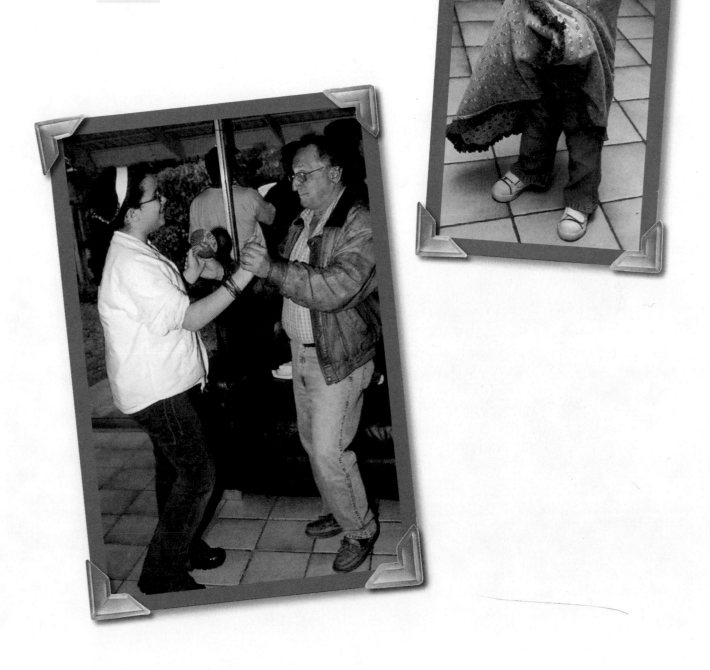

On Sundays we go to church with Grandma.
Then we all go to Aunt Martica and Uncle Miguel's
house. After lunch we play music and sing.

Uncle Miguel plays the double bass. Uncle Andrés plays the violin. Aunt Darleen plays the piano. Victor plays the clarinet and Mar Isabel plays the flute.

**STOP AND THINK**
**Author's Craft**  Music is part of Camila's story. Where in the story is music used?

We spend the rest of the day in the
backyard. The grown-ups play dominoes while
Uncle Andrés tells funny stories. Gabriela and I
sit on the porch and paint pictures.

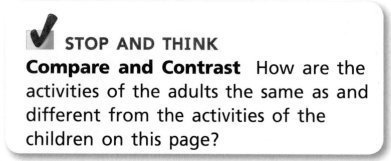
**STOP AND THINK**
**Compare and Contrast** How are the
activities of the adults the same as and
different from the activities of the
children on this page?

What I like best is when Papi takes us
fishing.  Most of the time my hook gets stuck
on a rock.  I can't wait to catch my first fish.

# Your Turn

## Family Visit

**Make a List**

What would it be like to spend a day with Camila and her family? Imagine that you could visit them. Make a list of three special things you would like to do. Then circle the one you would like to do first. PERSONAL RESPONSE

## Turn and Talk — Alike and Different

Work with a partner. Tell how families are alike and how they are different. Then think about what it would be like if all families were alike. Talk about your ideas.

COMPARE AND CONTRAST

# Poetry

✔ **TARGET VOCABULARY**

| | |
|---|---|
| remembered | stuck |
| porch | visit |
| crown | cousin |
| spend | piano |

**GENRE**

**Poetry** uses the sound of words to show pictures and feelings.

**TEXT FOCUS**

**Rhythm** is a pattern of beats, like music.

# Family Poetry

A family may have parents, brothers, sisters, grandparents, cousins, and more. People in a family visit one another and spend time together. Poets write about these remembered times. Listen to the rhythm of these family poems as you read them.

## Everybody Says

Everybody says

I look just like my mother.

Everybody says

I'm the image of Aunt Bee.

Everybody says

My nose is like my father's.

But *I* want to look like ME!

by Dorothy Aldis

# Abuelita's Lap

I know a place where I can sit
and tell about my day,
tell every color that I saw
from green to cactus gray.

I know a place where I can sit
and hear a favorite beat,
her heart and *cuentos* from the past,
the rhythms honey-sweet.

I know a place where I can sit
and listen to a star,
listen to its silent song
gliding from afar.

I know a place where I can sit
and hear the wind go by,
hearing it spinning round my house,
my whirling lullaby.

by Pat Mora

# What is a family?

What is a family?

Who is family?

Either a lot or a few is a family;

But whether there's ten or there's two in *your* family,

All of your family plus you is family!

by Mary Ann Hoberman

## Write a Family Poem

What do you like to do with your family?
Do you tell stories on the porch?
Do you play the piano and sing?
Write a poem about your family.
Try to use the words crown
and stuck in your poem.

# Making Connections

 **Text to Self**

**Select an Activity** What activity from *My Family* would you like to do with a family member? Explain your answer.

 **Text to Text**

**Write About Families** What is special about the families you have read about? Write a poem using what you have learned about families. Add details that tell about your senses.

 **Text to World**

**Connect to Social Studies** Camila's mother came from Cuba. Her father came from Puerto Rico. Now her family lives in Miami. Where could you look to find out more about these places? Make a plan.

# Grammar

**Complete Sentences** A **sentence** has both a **subject** and a **predicate**. The subject tells who or what did or does something. The predicate tells what the subject did or does.

| Subject | Predicate |
|---|---|
| Ana | sings. |
| My older brother | plays the drums. |

**Turn and Talk** **Work with a partner. Read each group of words aloud. Tell which groups of words are sentences.**

❶ Dad cooked.

❷ Harry's birthday.

❸ Ate three slices of cake!

❹ Jen and Bobbi danced.

**Sentence Fluency** When you write, use complete sentences. This will make your writing clearer.

**Not Complete Sentences**

My family.

Was Auntie Lu's birthday.

**Complete Sentences**

My family had a party.  It was Auntie Lu's birthday.

## Connect Grammar to Writing

**When you revise your friendly letter, fix any sentences that are not complete.  Add a subject or a predicate.**

# Write to Narrate

☑ **Voice** When you write a **friendly letter**, the voice of your letter shows what you are like.

Nestor drafted a letter to his uncle. Then he added words to make the letter sound more like the way he would talk to his uncle.

## Writing Traits Checklist

☑ **Organization**
Did I use the five parts of a friendly letter? Did I tell things in order?

☑ **Word Choice**
Did I use words that tell how I feel?

☑ **Voice**
Does the letter sound like me?

☑ **Conventions**
Did I capitalize and punctuate the date, greeting, and closing correctly?

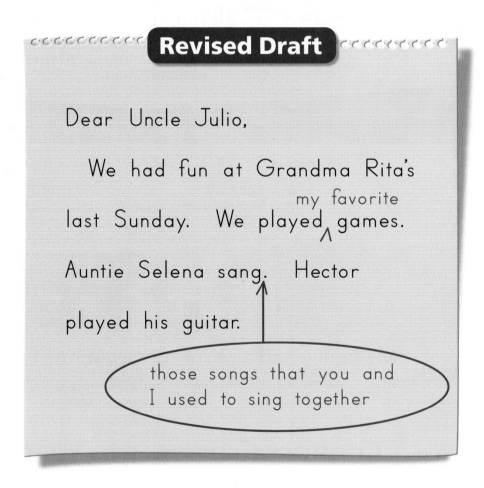

**Revised Draft**

Dear Uncle Julio,

We had fun at Grandma Rita's last Sunday. We played *my favorite* games.

Auntie Selena sang *those songs that you and I used to sing together*. Hector played his guitar.

September 24, 2011

Dear Uncle Julio,

We had fun at Grandma Rita's last Sunday. We played my favorite games. I wish you had been there. Auntie Selena sang those songs that you and I used to sing together. Hector played his guitar. Maybe you can come next time we go to Grandma Rita's. I miss you!

Love,
Nestor

I added words so my letter sounds like me and shows how I feel.

## Reading as a Writer

What did Nestor add to let you know how he feels? What can you add to your letter to show your thoughts and feelings?

Outdoor Adventures

## TARGET VOCABULARY

**woods**

**turned**

**tops**

**chipmunks**

**busy**

**picked**

**south**

**grew**

Vocabulary Reader

Context Cards

# Vocabulary in Context

- Read each **Context Card**.

- Talk about a picture. Use a different Vocabulary word from the one in the card.

### 1  woods

It is fun to walk in the woods. There are trees all around.

### 2  turned

These leaves turned red in the fall. They changed color.

### 3 tops

The tops of these trees look like they are pointing to the sky.

### 4 chipmunks

Chipmunks have brown fur with white and black stripes.

### 5 busy

When you are busy, you have a lot to do.

### 6 picked

These children picked apples from the trees at an apple farm.

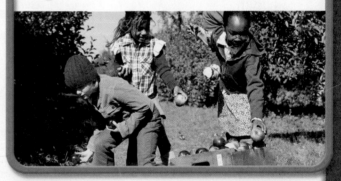

### 7 south

Many birds fly south for the winter. The weather is warmer there.

### 8 grew

This dog grew thicker fur for the winter. The thicker fur will keep the dog warm.

# Background

**A Busy Season** In many areas, fall is a busy time. It begins even before the first tree tops have turned from green to orange. Birds fly south for the winter. Apples and pumpkins are picked. The woods are busy, too. Chipmunks store nuts. Some deer even shed the antlers that they grew in the spring.

# Comprehension

✔ **TARGET SKILL** **Author's Purpose**

The author has a purpose for writing *Henry and Mudge Under the Yellow Moon*. Fill in a chart like this one with details as you read. Use them as clues to decide why the author wrote the selection.

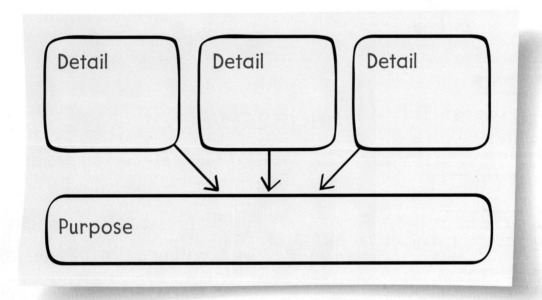

✔ **TARGET STRATEGY** **Analyze/Evaluate**

Think carefully about the story details and the author's purpose for writing *Henry and Mudge Under the Yellow Moon*. Use your own ideas to decide if the author has done a good job of writing this story.

## Main Selection

✔ **TARGET VOCABULARY**

| | |
|---|---|
| busy | turned |
| chipmunks | tops |
| south | grew |
| woods | picked |

✔ **TARGET SKILL**

**Author's Purpose** Tell why an author writes a book.

✔ **TARGET STRATEGY**

**Analyze/Evaluate** Tell how you feel about the text, and why.

**GENRE**

**Realistic fiction** is a story that could happen in real life.

**MEET THE AUTHOR**

# Cynthia Rylant

Cynthia Rylant loves animals, which is why you will find many in her books. She likes to take walks with her dogs. "Sometimes we have adventures," she says. "Someone will fall into a lake or someone will meet a raccoon—but mostly we just have lovely, quiet walks."

**MEET THE ILLUSTRATOR**

# Suçie Stevenson

Suçie Stevenson has drawn the pictures for most of the Henry and Mudge books. Her brother's Great Dane, Jake, gave her the idea for Mudge. Suçie Stevenson takes her own dogs for walks on the beach. She likes seeing them swim to fetch balls.

# HENRY and MUDGE
## Under the Yellow Moon

by Cynthia Rylant

Illustrated by Suçie Stevenson

**Essential Question**

Why might an author write a story?

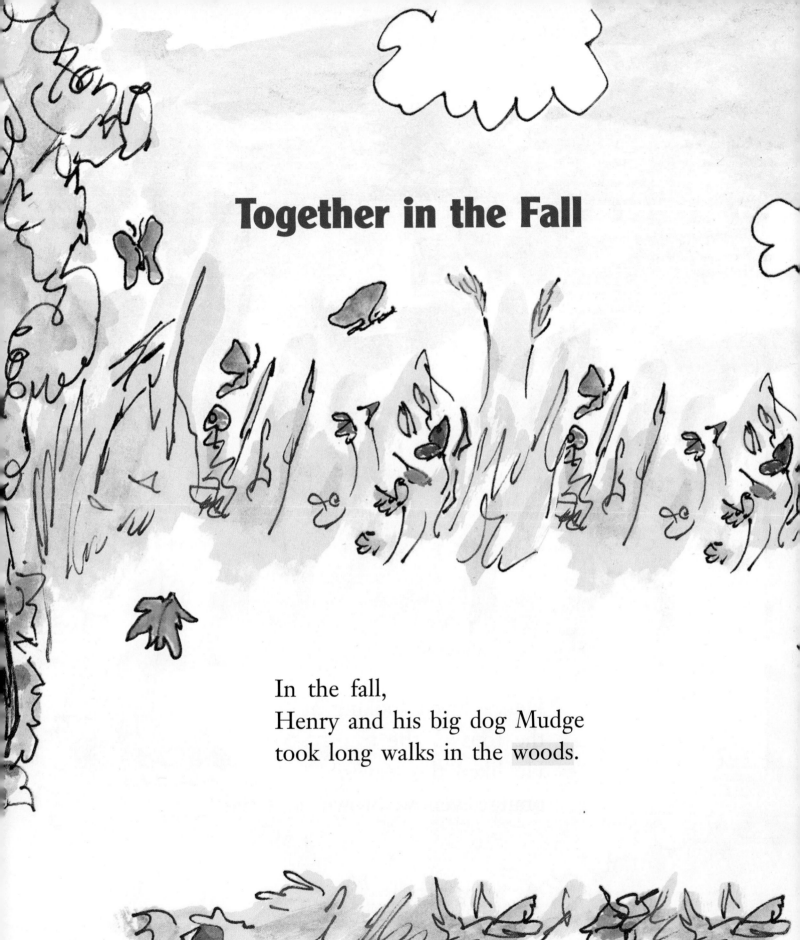

# Together in the Fall

In the fall,
Henry and his big dog Mudge
took long walks in the woods.

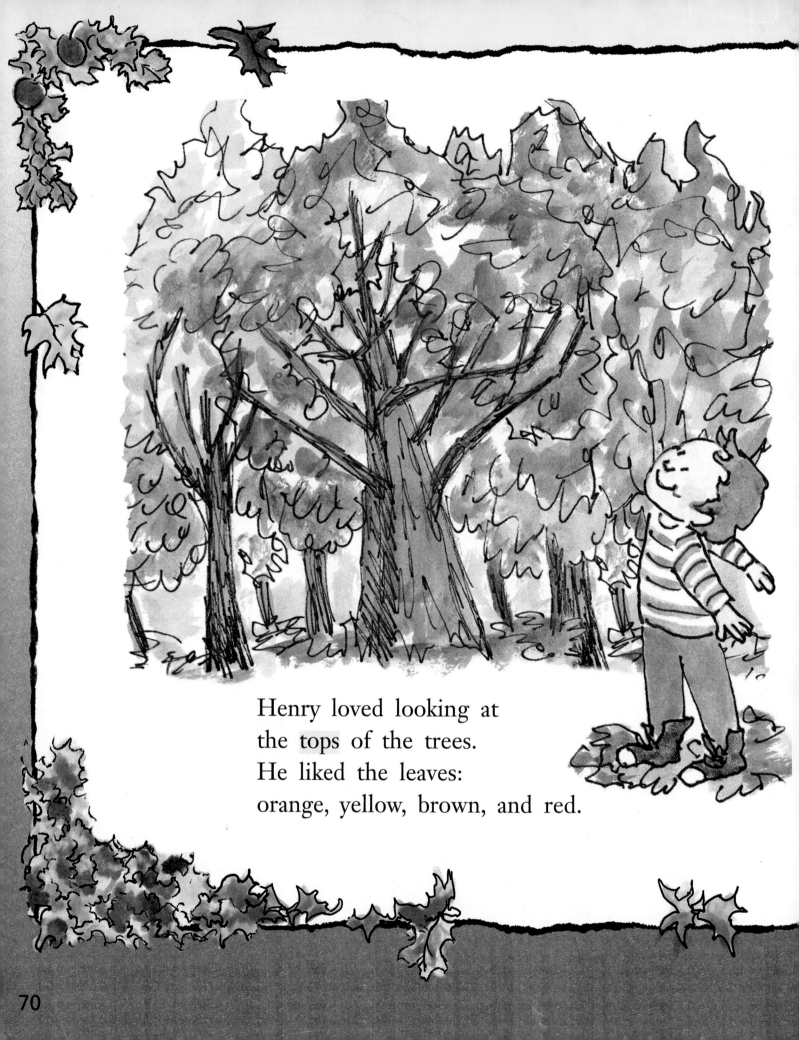

Henry loved looking at
the tops of the trees.
He liked the leaves:
orange, yellow, brown, and red.

Mudge loved sniffing at the ground.
And he liked the leaves, too.
He always ate a few.

**✔ STOP AND THINK**
**Author's Purpose** Why does the author show that Henry and Mudge are good friends?

In the fall,
Henry liked counting the birds
flying south.
Mudge liked
watching for busy chipmunks.

Since one was a boy
and the other was a dog,
they never did things
just the same way.

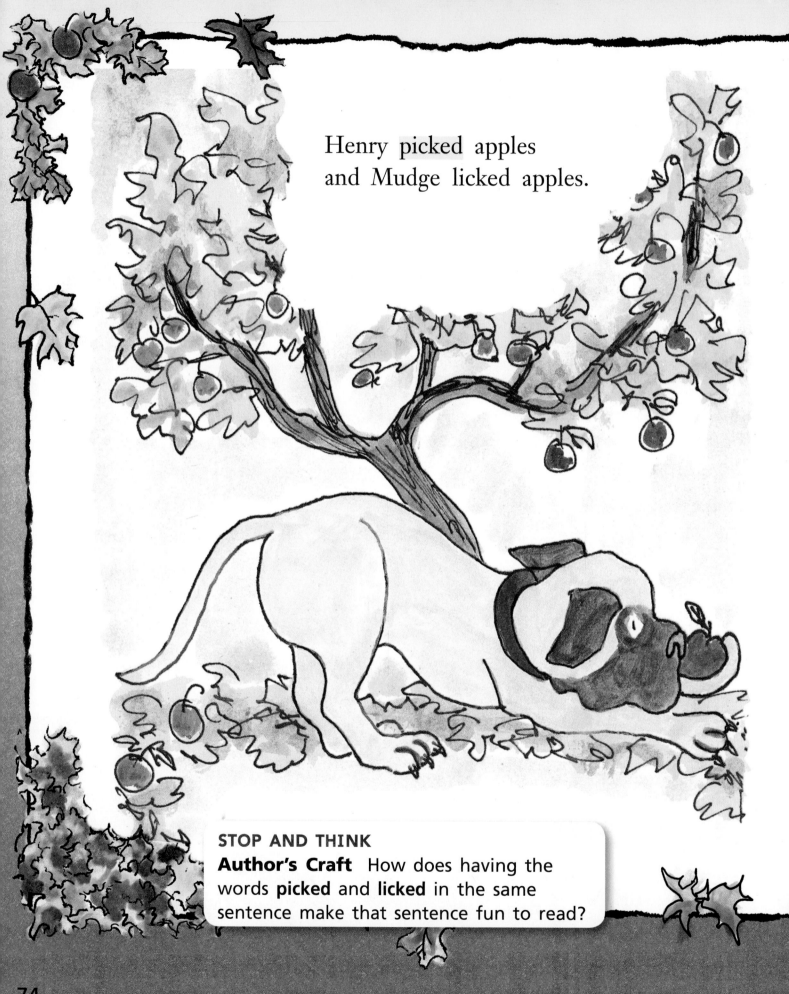

Henry picked apples
and Mudge licked apples.

**STOP AND THINK**
**Author's Craft** How does having the
words **picked** and **licked** in the same
sentence make that sentence fun to read?

Henry put on a coat
and Mudge grew one.
And when the fall wind blew,
Henry's ears turned red
and Mudge's ears
turned inside out.

But one thing about them
was the same.
In the fall
Henry and Mudge liked
being together,
most of all.

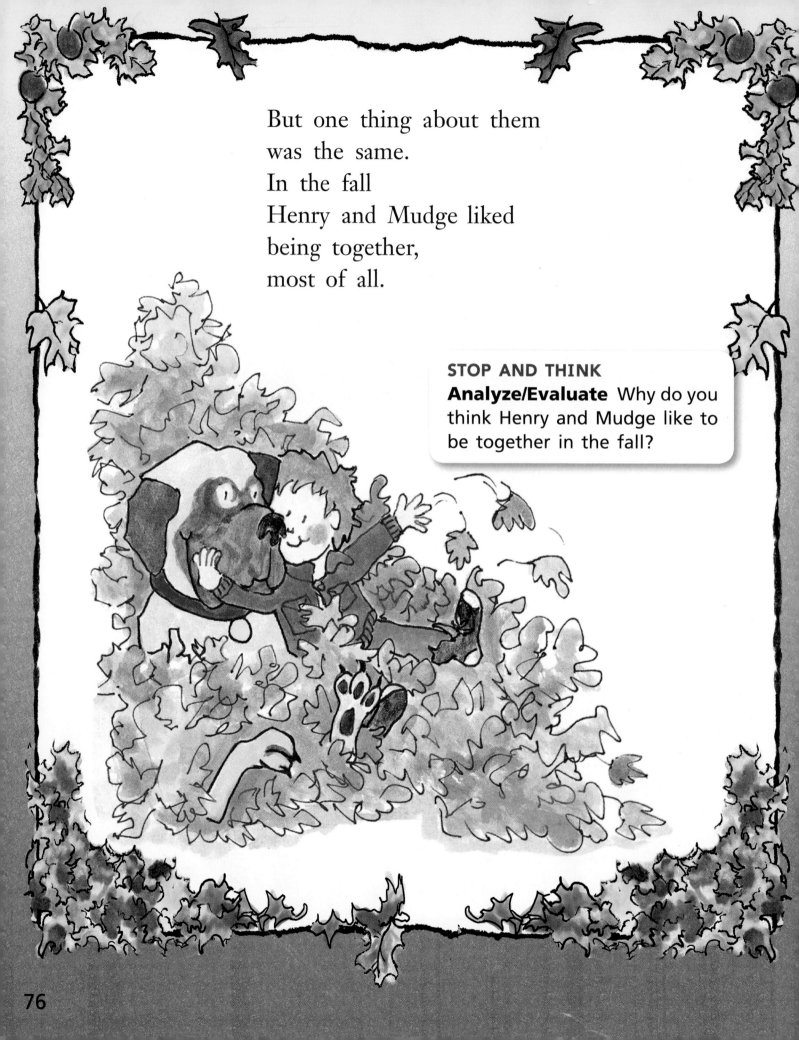

**STOP AND THINK**
**Analyze/Evaluate** Why do you think Henry and Mudge like to be together in the fall?

**Walk in the Woods**

### Act It Out

Picture yourself in the woods on a fall day. What would you do? What might you see or hear? Act out one of these things. Have a partner guess what you are doing, seeing, or hearing. Then switch roles. PARTNERS

**Turn and Talk** **Author's Purpose**

Think about why the author wrote *Henry and Mudge Under the Yellow Moon.* With a partner, find words and pictures from the story that show the author's purpose. Share your ideas. AUTHOR'S PURPOSE

# Technology

Outdoor
Adventures

✔ **TARGET VOCABULARY**

| | |
|---|---|
| woods | busy |
| turned | picked |
| tops | south |
| chipmunks | grew |

**GENRE**

**Informational text** gives facts about a topic.

**TEXT FOCUS**

An **e-mail** is an electronic message sent from one person to another. As you read, find the different parts of an e-mail.

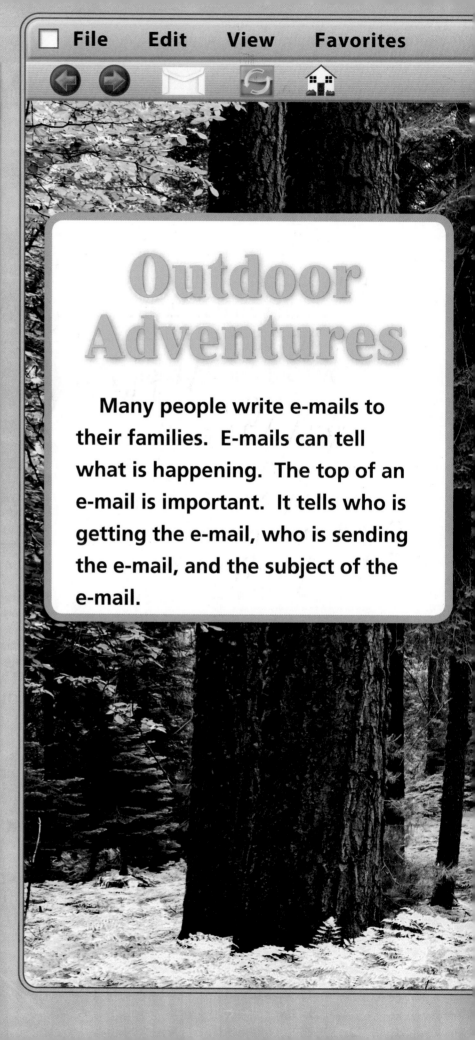

# Outdoor Adventures

Many people write e-mails to their families. E-mails can tell what is happening. The top of an e-mail is important. It tells who is getting the e-mail, who is sending the e-mail, and the subject of the e-mail.

search

To: Abuelita

From: Lola

Subject:    Animal Hunt

Dear Abuelita,

   We are very busy in school this week.  Each day
we are walking in the woods.  Today we found
animals.  We saw chipmunks storing acorns for the
winter.  I spotted a hare that already grew its winter
coat.  It was very furry!  We also saw birds flying
south.  I took a picture for you.

Write back!

Lola

**Geese fly in a V shape.  They take turns flying
in the front.  This helps them fly longer.**

To: Lola

From: Abuelita

Subject:　Plant Hunt

Dear Lola,

　　Your walks at school sound like fun. I have been taking walks, too. I look at plants in the woods. The tree tops have turned from green to red. Leaves cannot last through the cold winter. They are starting to drop off. I picked a few leaves to take home. Here are some pictures for you.

Talk to you soon,

Abuelita

**Trees that have needles do not change colors. They can survive the winter.**

**When leaves turn colors, they stop making food for the tree.**

# Making Connections

 **Text to Self**

**Discuss an Activity** Henry and Mudge loved walking in the leaves. Do you enjoy walking in the leaves? Discuss what you like and don't like about it.

 **Text to Text**

**Compare and Contrast** Think about how the two *Henry and Mudge* stories you read are alike and different. Write sentences that tell what happens in each story. Tell how the settings are alike and different.

 **Text to World**

**Connect to Science** Go for a nature walk in your community. Draw and label interesting things you see. Make a list of questions you have about anything you see with a partner.

Maple Leaf

What makes leaves change from green to red?

# Grammar

**Statements and Questions** Statements and questions are types of **sentences.** All sentences begin with a capital letter. A **statement** tells something. It ends with a period. A **question** asks something. It ends with a question mark.

**Academic Language**

sentences

statement

question

| Statements | Questions |
|---|---|
| I live near the woods.<br>Brendan sat by the pond. | Do you live near the woods?<br>Who sat by the pond? |

**Try This!** **Decide whether each sentence is a statement or a question. Write each sentence correctly.**

1 where do you like to walk

2 we hike up the hills

3 may I come with you

4 i will bring my jacket

**Sentence Fluency** Using different kinds of sentences makes your writing more fun to read. You can change one kind of sentence to another by moving or adding words.

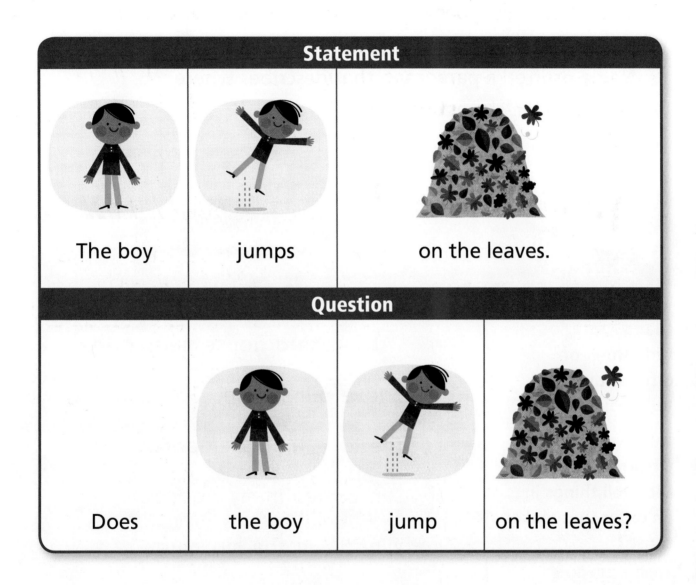

## Connect Grammar to Writing

**When you revise your sentences that describe, try using different kinds of sentences to make your writing more interesting.**

# Write to Narrate

✔ **Word Choice** You can make a **description** more interesting when you use sense words to tell how things look, feel, smell, sound, and taste.

Nadia drafted a paragraph that describes where she lives. Later, she added sense words.

## Writing Traits Checklist

✔ **Ideas**
Did I think of different ways to tell about where I live?

✔ **Organization**
Did I tell things in an order that makes sense?

✔ **Word Choice**
Did I use sense words to tell more?

✔ **Sentence Fluency**
Did I use different kinds of sentences?

## Revised Draft

little green      big blue
I live in a house near a lake.
          ∧                    ∧

I love our house.  You can see
              I love to feel the warm
the lake from our porch.  ~~The~~
when it
sun ∧comes in my bedroom

window in the morning.

84

# My House

## by Nadia Krimsky

I live in a little green house near a big blue lake. I love our house. You can see the lake from our porch. I love to feel the warm sun when it comes in my bedroom window in the morning. Do you know what wakes me up? The birds start chirping. I smell the pancakes my dad makes. They taste so good that I always ask for more!

> I used sense words to tell the reader more about how things look, feel, smell, taste, and sound.

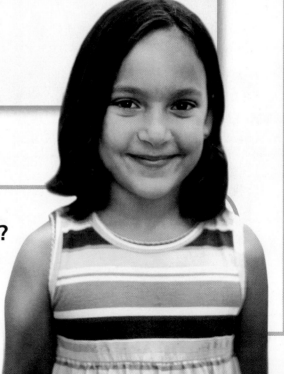

## Reading as a Writer

**Which sense words did Nadia add? What sense words can you add to your story?**

✓ **TARGET VOCABULARY**

**insects**

**dangerous**

**scare**

**sticky**

**rotten**

**screaming**

**breeze**

**judge**

Vocabulary
Reader

Context
Cards

# Vocabulary in Context

● Read each **Context Card**.

● Ask a question that uses one of the Vocabulary words.

**1**    **insects**

Ants, flies, and bees are all insects. They all have six legs.

**2**    **dangerous**

Be careful! A bee sting can be dangerous. It makes some people sick.

### 3 scare

Cockroaches will run away if you scare them. They frighten easily.

### 4 sticky

A spider web is sticky. Bugs get caught, and they can't fly away.

### 5 rotten

A housefly eats rotten, or spoiled, food.

### 6 screaming

If you see a wasp, walk away quietly. Don't run away screaming.

### 7 breeze

A ladybug came in when a breeze blew open the window curtains.

### 8 judge

Look carefully before you judge, or decide, what this picture shows.

# Background

**Spiders** Spiders are not insects. Spiders have eight legs. Insects have six. Some spiders spin sticky webs to catch food. Their webs are so strong a breeze will not break them. Spiders may scare people and cause a lot of screaming, but most are not dangerous. In fact, spiders are helpful because they eat harmful insects. They do not eat rotten things. Do not judge spiders based on the few that bite.

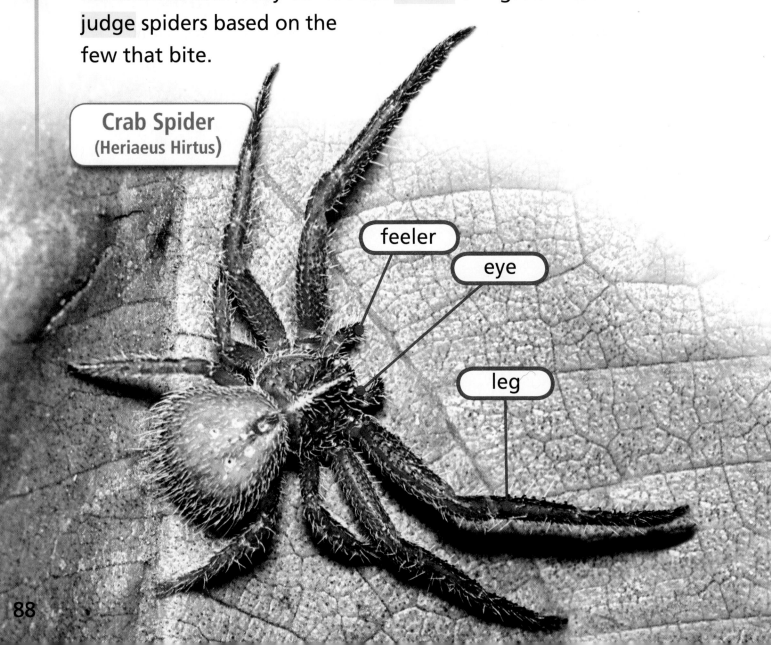

**Crab Spider**
(Heriaeus Hirtus)

feeler

eye

leg

# Comprehension

✔ TARGET SKILL **Cause and Effect**

Some people see a spider and get scared. The two events are linked. Seeing the spider is the cause. Becoming scared is the effect. As you read, use a chart like this one to list some of the causes and effects in *Diary of a Spider*. Tell what happens and why.

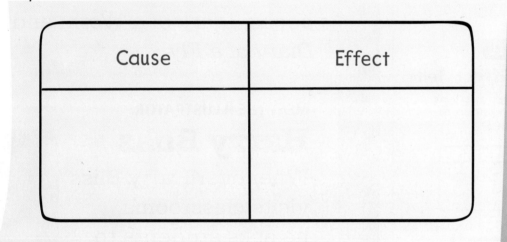

| Cause | Effect |
|-------|--------|
|       |        |

✔ TARGET STRATEGY **Summarize**

Use your chart to help you summarize, or briefly retell in your own words, some important story events and their causes.

### ✔ TARGET VOCABULARY

| | |
|---|---|
| insects | rotten |
| dangerous | screaming |
| scare | breeze |
| sticky | judge |

### ✔ TARGET SKILL

**Cause and Effect** Tell how one event makes another happen.

### ✔ TARGET STRATEGY

**Summarize** Stop to tell important events as you read.

### GENRE

Humorous fiction is a story that is written to make the reader laugh.

**MEET THE AUTHOR**

# Doreen Cronin

Two spiders have moved into Doreen Cronin's office, but she says she cannot bring herself to get rid of them. If you like *Diary of a Spider*, check out Ms. Cronin's other books, *Diary of a Worm* and *Diary of a Fly*.

**MEET THE ILLUSTRATOR**

# Harry Bliss

Whenever Harry Bliss visits classrooms, he asks students to scribble on the board. He then turns their scribbles into an animal, a tree, or a cartoon character. This scribble game helps kids use their imagination.

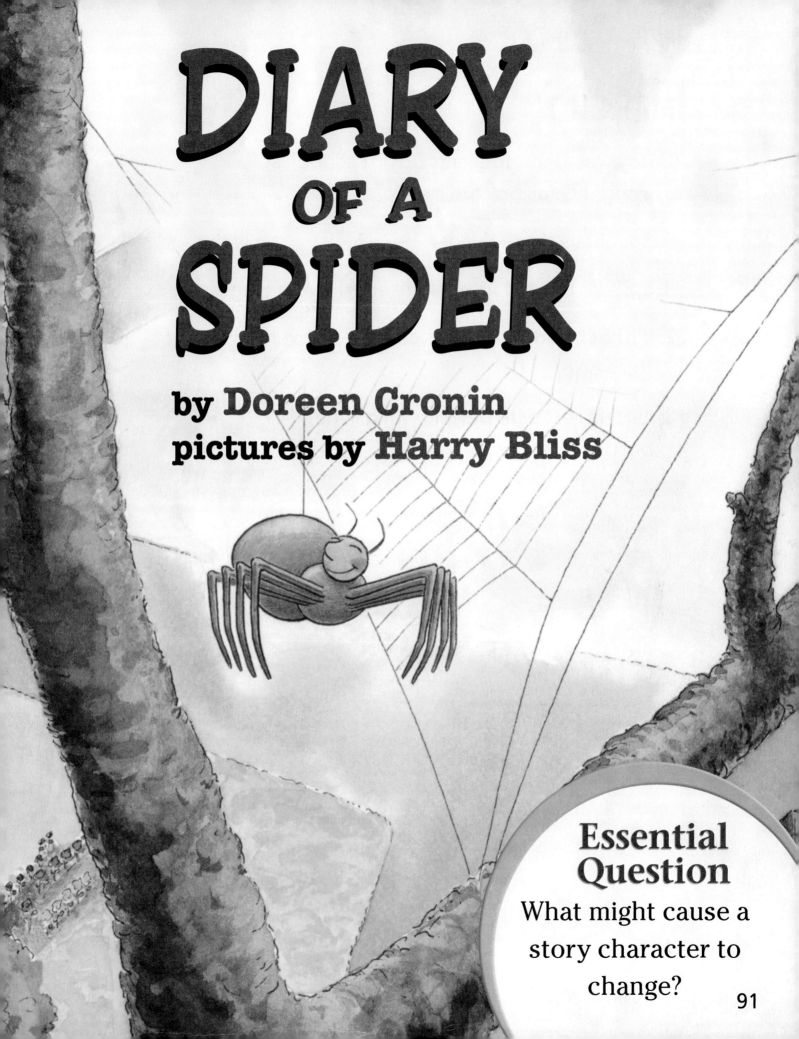

# DIARY OF A SPIDER

## by Doreen Cronin
## pictures by Harry Bliss

**Essential Question**

What might cause a story character to change?

# MARCH 1

Today was Grandparents Day at school, so I brought Grampa with me.

He taught us three things:

1. Spiders are not insects—insects have six legs.

2. Without spiders, insects could take over the world.

3. Butterflies taste better with a little barbecue sauce.

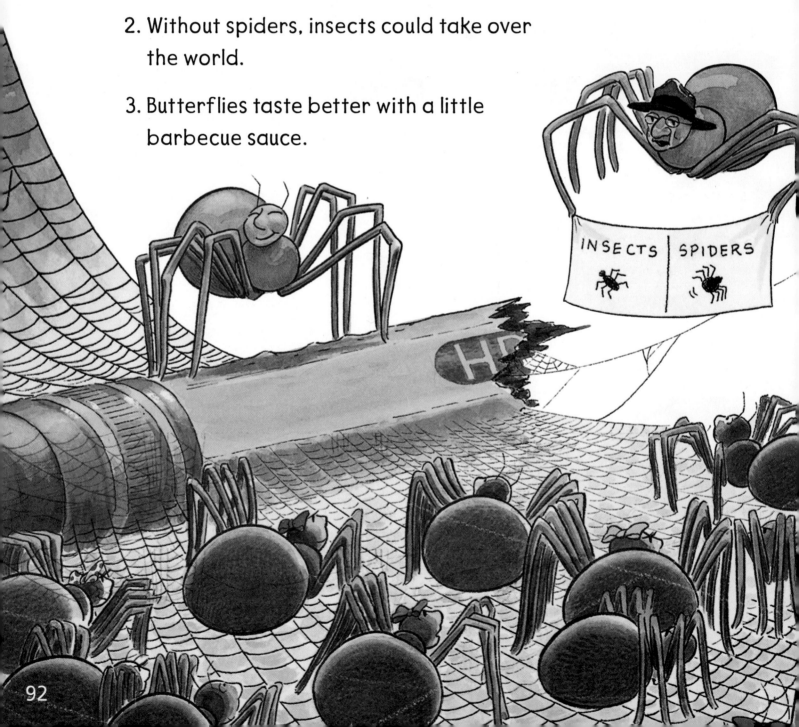

# MARCH 16

Grampa says that in his day, flies and spiders did not get along.

Things are different now.

# MARCH 29

Today in gym class we learned how to catch the wind so we could travel to faraway places.

94

When I got home, I made up flash cards so I
could practice:

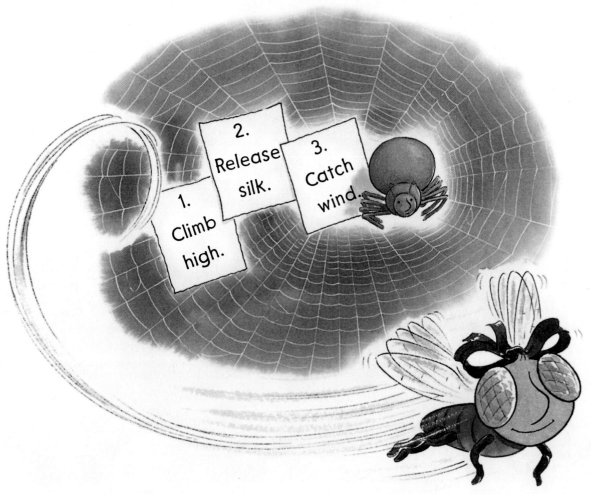

Fly made up her own flash card:

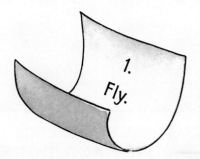

I'm starting to see why
Grampa doesn't like her.

**STOP AND THINK**
**Summarize** What does Spider do
to learn to fly to faraway places?

**APRIL 1**

I went to the park with my sister today. We tried the seesaw.

It didn't work.

✔️ **STOP AND THINK**
**Cause and Effect** Why does the seesaw not work? Use the illustration to help you answer.

We tried the tire swing.

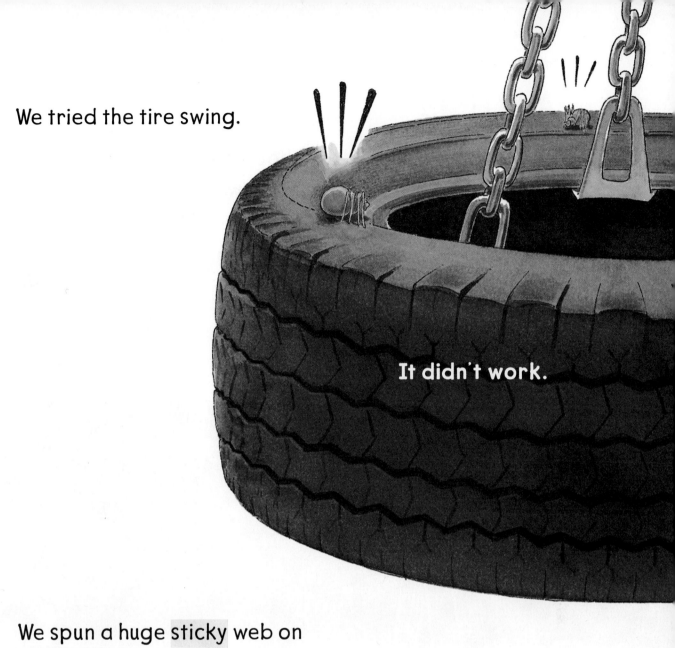

It didn't work.

We spun a huge sticky web on
the water fountain.

That worked.

EEEEEEK!

99

# APRIL 12

Today was Safety Day at school. We learned that vacuums eat spiderwebs and are very, very dangerous. If we hear a vacuum, we should Stop, Drop, and Run.

STOP WHAT WE'RE DOING. DROP FROM THE WEB. RUN LIKE CRAZY.

# APRIL 13

We had a vacuum drill today.
I stopped what I was doing.

Forgot where I was going.

And ran screaming from the room.

We're having another drill tomorrow.

## APRIL 17

I'm sleeping over at Worm's house tonight. I hope they don't have leaves and rotten tomatoes for dinner again.

## MAY 7

Mom said I was getting too big for my own skin. So I molted.

That is soooo gross!

# MAY 8

Today was show-and-tell. So I brought in my old skin. My teacher called on it to lead the Pledge of Allegiance.

# JUNE 5

Daddy Longlegs made fun of Fly because she eats with her feet. Now she won't come out of her tree house.

I'm going to find him and give him a piece of my mind!

# JUNE 6

I found Daddy Longlegs. He's a lot bigger than
I thought he was.

I gave him a piece of my lunch instead.

# JUNE 7

Fly's tree house blew away in the wind today.

So did Grampa.

# JUNE 18

I got a postcard from Grampa today:

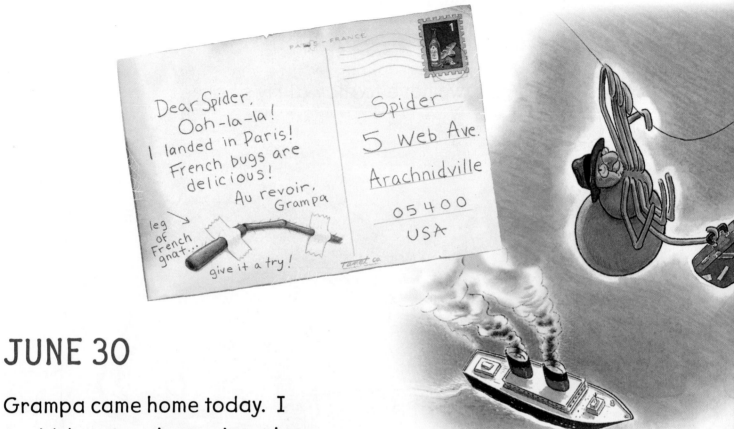

# JUNE 30

Grampa came home today. I couldn't wait to hear about how he rode the winds all the way over the ocean!

Turns out, he caught a breeze to the airport and napped in first class.

# JULY 2

Fly came over to play today.  She got stuck in our web, and her mom had to come get her.

Grampa laughed a little too hard.

From now on, we have to play at Fly's house.

# JULY 9

Today was my birthday. Grampa decided I was old enough to know the secret to a long, happy life:

Never fall asleep in a shoe.

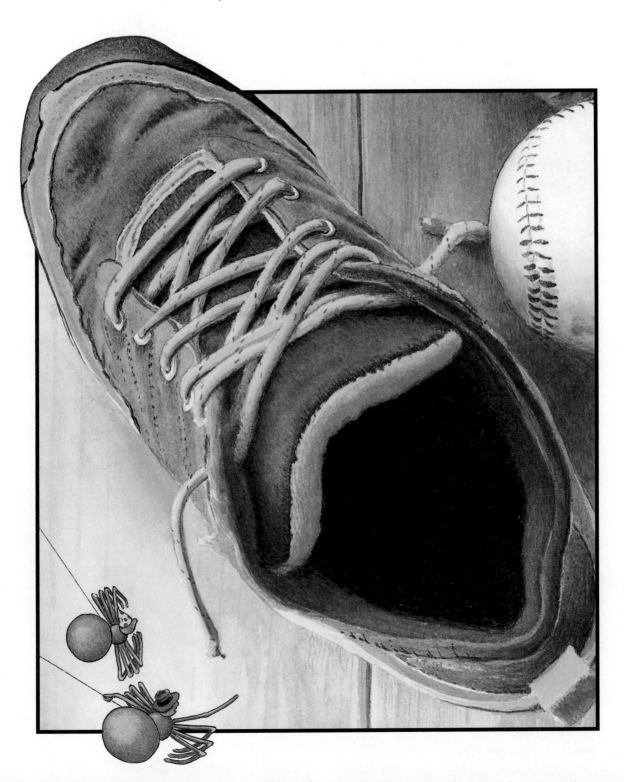

# JULY 16

Things I scare:

1. Fly's mom

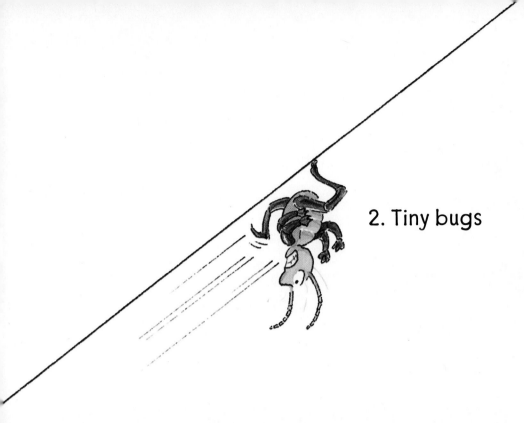

## 2. Tiny bugs

## 3. People using water fountains at the park

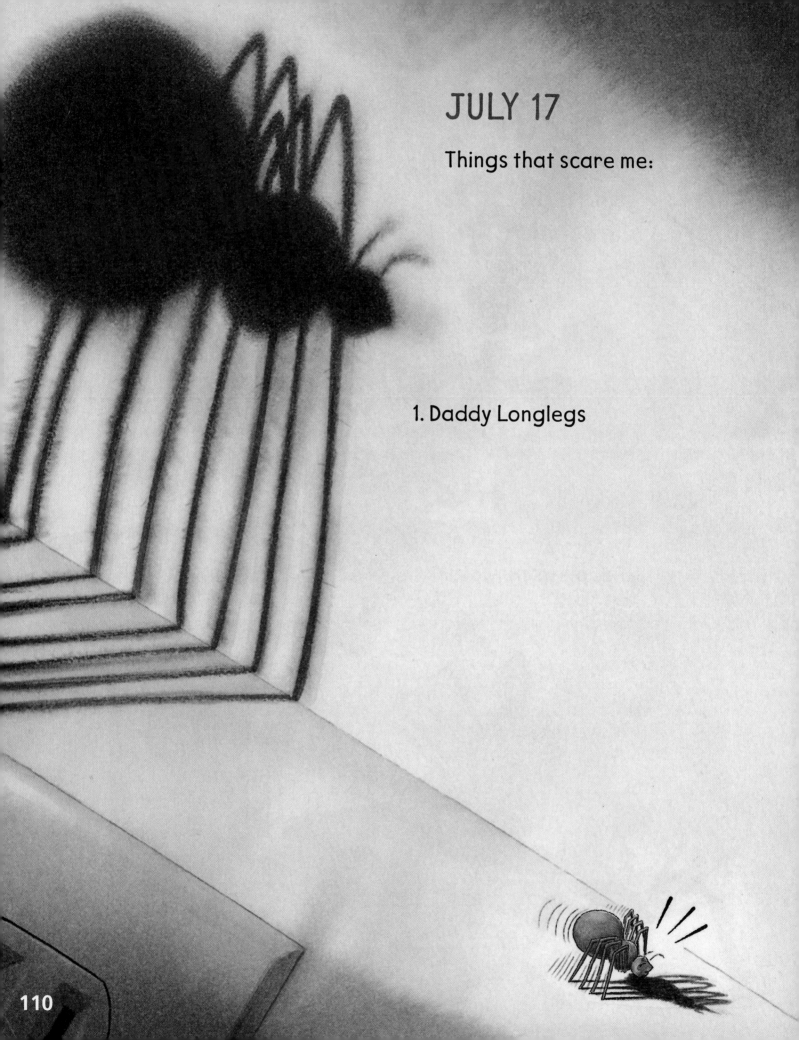

# JULY 17

Things that scare me:

1. Daddy Longlegs

## 2. Vacuums

## 3. People with big feet

# AUGUST 1

I wish that people wouldn't judge all spiders based on the few spiders that bite.

I know if we took the time to get to know each other, we would get along just fine.

Just like me and Fly.

**STOP AND THINK**
**Author's Craft** The story is funny because Spider seems like a person. How does the author make Spider seem like a person?

## Your Turn

### Dear Diary

**Write a Diary Entry**

If you could be a spider for a day, what would you do?  Write a diary entry telling about your day.  Start the first sentence with *Today I* _____.  Draw pictures to go with your sentences.  PERSONAL RESPONSE

### Turn and Talk — Making Friends

By the end of the story, Spider has learned many important things.  What events in the story cause this to happen?  Work with a partner.  List story details that show how Spider learns those lessons.  CAUSE AND EFFECT

1. Spider goes to school.
2.

# Traditional Tales

✔ **TARGET VOCABULARY**

| | |
|---|---|
| insects | rotten |
| dangerous | screaming |
| scare | breeze |
| sticky | judge |

**GENRE**

A **fable** is a short story in which a character learns a lesson.

**TEXT FOCUS**

The **moral** of a fable is the lesson that a character learns. As you read, find the moral of the story.

# A Swallow and a Spider

## A FABLE FROM AESOP

retold by Sheila Higginson

**Cast of Characters**

| Narrator | Spider | Swallow |
|---|---|---|

**Narrator:** A spider sat in her sticky web, waiting for dinner.

**Spider:** I hope some insects will stop by soon.

**Narrator:** Spider heard the buzz of flies floating in the breeze.

**Swallow:** Look at those juicy flies!

**Narrator:** Before the flies could reach her web, they were scooped up in Swallow's beak.

**Spider:** Swallow is a pest! I will show him what I can do!

**Narrator:** Spider worked for a whole week. She spun a huge web.

**Spider:** Swallow doesn't scare me. I may be small, but I am dangerous, too!

**Narrator:** Spider put some berries in the middle of the web.

**Spider:** Swallow will smell these berries. Then he will get stuck in my net!

**Narrator:** Spider watched and waited, waited and watched.

**Swallow:** I smell something delicious. Those berries are just waiting for me!

**Spider:** Those berries aren't for you! Don't eat them! They are rotten.

**Narrator:** Swallow scooped up the berries and flew right through spider's web! He didn't even hear spider screaming at him!

**Spider:** I can judge what I am good at. I am good at building webs to catch insects, but I am not a good bird-catcher. I'll go back to my web to wait for a juicy fly.

**Narrator:** The moral of the story is, "A wise man will not try something he is not able to do."

# Making Connections

 **Text to Self**

**Different Ending** Think about how *A Swallow and a Spider* could have ended differently. Write the new ending as a play and act it out.

 **Text to Text**

**Compare and Contrast** *Diary of a Spider* and *A Swallow and a Spider* are both about spiders. Make a list of ways they are alike and different.

 **Text to World**

**Connect to Science** Make a poster to teach your classmates about real spiders. Use the two stories you just read or science books to help you.

# Grammar

**What Is a Noun?**  A **noun** is a word that names a person, animal, place, or thing.

| People | Animals |
|--------|---------|
| grandfather | spider |
| girl | fly |
| friend | bird |

| Places | Things |
|--------|--------|
| home | web |
| school | vacuum |
| park | tomato |

**Turn and Talk**  **Work with a partner.  Find the noun in each sentence.  Tell whether it is a person, animal, place, or thing.**

❶ Our swing did not move.

❷ The worm sleeps.

❸ My teacher is nice.

❹ The airport is big.

**Word Choice** When you write, use exact nouns to paint a picture in your reader's mind. An exact noun gives more information about an animal, a person, a place, or a thing.

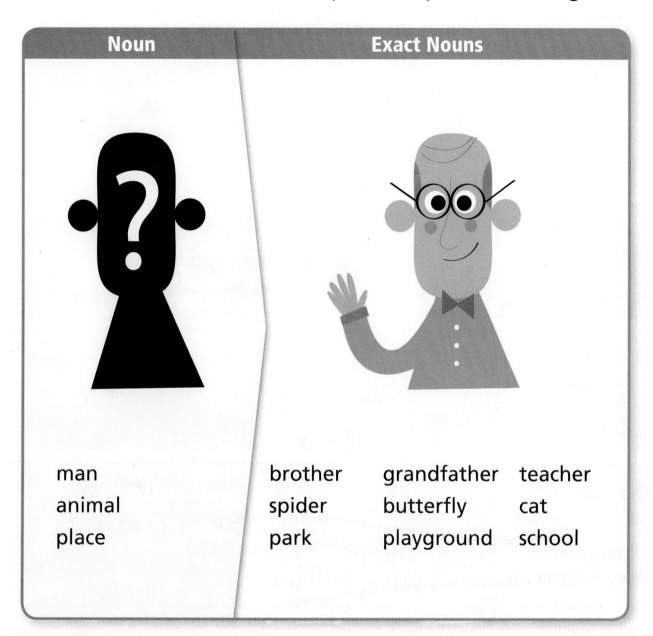

| Noun | Exact Nouns | | |
|------|------|------|------|
| man | brother | grandfather | teacher |
| animal | spider | butterfly | cat |
| place | park | playground | school |

## Connect Grammar to Writing

**As you revise your true story next week, look for nouns you could replace with exact nouns.**

# Write to Narrate

✔ **Ideas** The main idea is the most important part of a **true story**. Everything in your story should connect to the main idea.

Raj made a list of ideas for his true story. He decided which idea would make the best story. Then he made an idea web for his true story.

## Writing Process Checklist

▶ **Prewrite**

✔ What is the most important idea of my story?

✔ What details tell about what happened?

✔ Do all the parts of the story connect to the main idea?

✔ Is there anything that doesn't belong?

**Draft**

**Revise**

**Edit**

**Publish and Share**

## Exploring a Topic

basketball

my sister's cat

video games

me in the author's chair

why I don't like to practice piano

✔ **TARGET VOCABULARY**

**wonderful**

**noises**

**quiet**

**sprinkled**

**share**

**noticed**

**bursting**

**suddenly**

Vocabulary
Reader

Context
Cards

# Vocabulary in Context

- Read each **Context Card**.

- Tell a story about two pictures, using the Vocabulary words.

**1**  **wonderful**

Pets are wonderful. They make very good friends.

**2**  **noises**

Big dogs bark loudly. Small dogs do not make such loud noises.

**3** **quiet**

A lizard is a very quiet pet. It does not make a sound.

**4** **sprinkled**

The fish food was lightly sprinkled on top of the water.

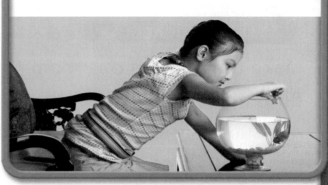

**5** **share**

These kittens all share a bowl of food.

**6** **noticed**

This pet rabbit noticed, or looked carefully, at the carrot held for it to eat.

**7** **bursting**

Look at this crowded basket. It is bursting with puppies!

**8** **suddenly**

A pet parrot might surprise you if it suddenly says a word.

# Background

**Classroom Pets** Which animals make the quietest classroom pets? They are not birds. Birds make loud noises. The classroom can be quiet, and suddenly a pet bird is bursting into song. They are not guinea pigs. When they run around, their wheels squeak and their cages rattle. The quietest pets are fish. They are so quiet they may not get noticed. Fish quietly eat food sprinkled in their tank. Why not share the classroom with wonderful pet fish?

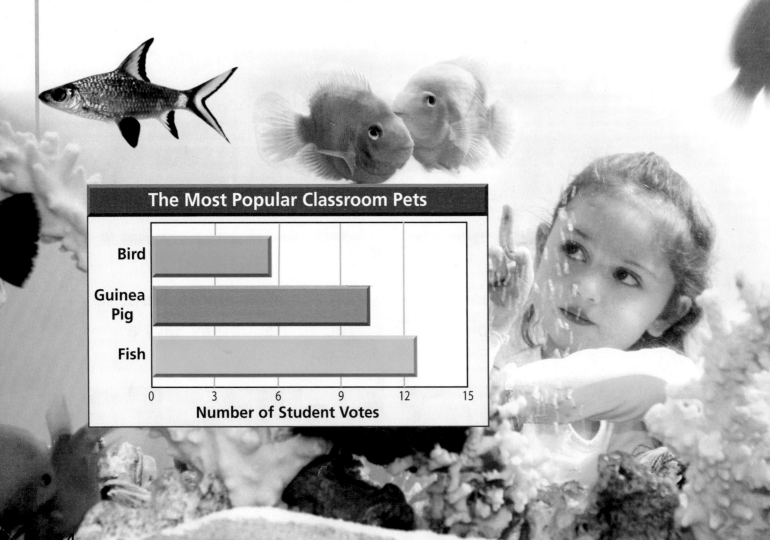

### The Most Popular Classroom Pets

| | |
|---|---|
| Bird | |
| Guinea Pig | |
| Fish | |

0  3  6  9  12  15

**Number of Student Votes**

# Comprehension

**✔ TARGET SKILL** **Story Structure**

Where does *Teacher's Pets* take place, and who is in it? What problem does a character face, and how is it solved? Use a story map like this one to tell the main parts of the story. List details about the setting, characters, and plot.

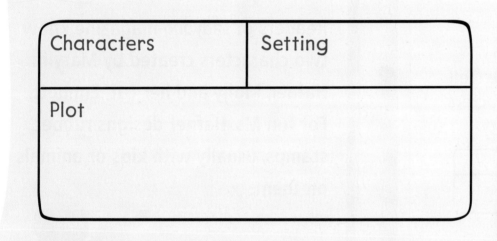

| Characters | Setting |
|------------|---------|
| Plot | |

**✔ TARGET STRATEGY** **Visualize**

Visualizing, or drawing pictures in your mind, makes stories come to life. Use story details to visualize what happens at different parts of the story.

### ✓ TARGET VOCABULARY

| | |
|---|---|
| wonderful | share |
| noises | noticed |
| quiet | bursting |
| sprinkled | suddenly |

### ✓ TARGET SKILL

**Story Structure** Tell the setting, characters, and plot in a story.

| | |
|---|---|
| | |

### ✓ TARGET STRATEGY

**Visualize** Picture what is happening as you read.

### GENRE

**Realistic fiction** is a story that could happen in real life. Set a purpose for reading based on the genre.

**MEET THE AUTHOR**
## Dayle Ann Dodds

Dayle Ann Dodds received a very special honor in 2007. Her book *Teacher's Pets* was read to hundreds of kids on the lawn of the White House during the annual Easter egg roll.

**MEET THE ILLUSTRATOR**
## Marylin Hafner

Readers of *Ladybug* magazine know two characters created by Marylin Hafner, Molly and her cat, Emmett. For fun Ms. Hafner designs rubber stamps, usually with kids or animals on them.

# Teacher's Pets

by **Dayle Ann Dodds**

illustrated by **Marylin Hafner**

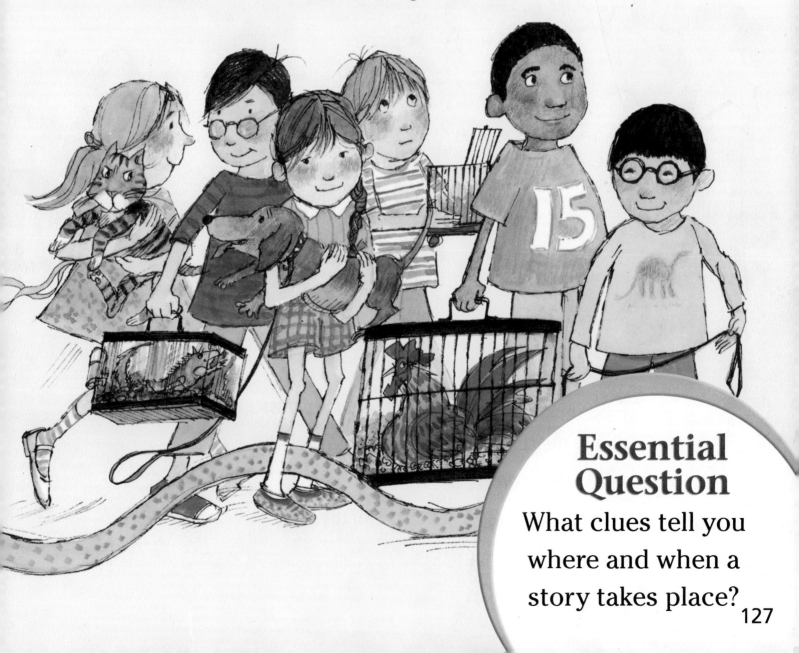

**Essential Question**

What clues tell you where and when a story takes place?

127

Monday was sharing day in Miss Fry's class.

"You may bring something special," said Miss Fry.

"May we share a pet?" Winston asked.

"Yes," said Miss Fry. "But just for the day."

On Monday, Winston brought in his pet rooster.

"I call him Red. He eats corn, and he crows. The neighbors say he crows too much."

"What a wonderful pet," said Miss Fry. "We're happy he can visit us today."

But that afternoon, after all the children had left, there
was Red, still sitting on his roost near Miss Fry's desk.

She sprinkled corn in Red's dish, then locked the door and went home to her quiet little house.

On Tuesday, Winston told Miss Fry, "The neighbors wonder if Red can stay at school for a while."

"Of course," said Miss Fry. "How lucky for us."

The next Monday was Patrick's turn. "My tarantula's name is Vincent. He likes to eat bugs and hide inside my mother's slippers."

"What a wonderful pet," said Miss Fry. "Don't forget to take Vincent home with you at the end of the day."

**STOP AND THINK**
**Author's Craft** What does "pet" mean above? What else can "pet" mean, as in a "teacher's pet"?

But that afternoon, after all the children had left, there was Vincent, still sitting in his jar on Miss Fry's desk. She gave Vincent a big juicy bug, sprinkled corn on Red's dish, then locked the door and went home to her quiet little house.

On Tuesday, Patrick told Miss Fry, "My mother says Vincent likes her slippers too much. We're wondering if he can stay at school for a few days."

"Of course," said Miss Fry. "How lucky for us."

The next week, Roger brought in his cricket.

"His name is Moe," said Roger. "He eats leaves from the garden and sings *chirrup-chirrup* all night long."

"What a wonderful pet," said Miss Fry.

That afternoon, after all the children had left, Miss Fry noticed Moe sitting in his box on the table. Miss Fry looked at Moe. He almost seemed to smile. "Welcome to our class, Moe."

✔ **STOP AND THINK**
**Story Structure** How does Winston start a big change in Miss Fry's classroom?

Right before her eyes, he did a huge somersault—up, up in the air. "Bravo!" said Miss Fry.

She gave fresh green leaves to Moe and a big juicy bug to Vincent, sprinkled corn in Red's dish, then locked the door and went home to her quiet little house.

The next day, Roger said to Miss Fry, "My mother says Moe chirps too much.".

"He's welcome to visit as long as he likes," said Miss Fry.

And so it went.

Alia shared her pet goat named Gladys. It said *Baaaaa!* and ate her sister's homework.

Amanda shared her pet dachshund. It liked to chew bones and the pillows on her aunt Judy's new sofa.

Jerry brought in his pet boa constrictor. It never made a sound. No one knew exactly what it liked to eat, but Jerry said his father's expensive tropical fish had suddenly disappeared one day.

There was Megan's cat,

Mitchell's mice,

Daniel's ducks,

and Tom's iguana.

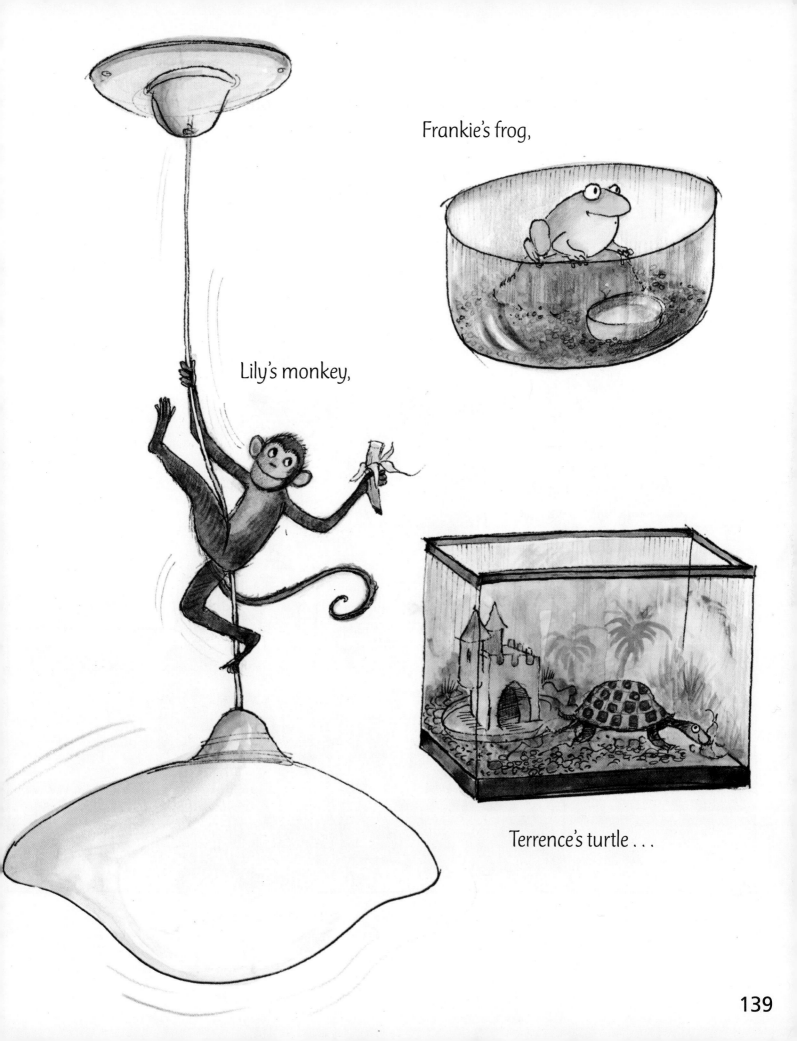

Frankie's frog,

Lily's monkey,

Terrence's turtle . . .

and something square and fuzzy that Avery brought in.

"It looks like a kitchen sponge," said Bruce. "A *really old* kitchen sponge."

"It's my pet," said Avery, and that was that.

Before long, Miss Fry's classroom was bursting with the happy noises of all the children's pets.

**STOP AND THINK**
**Visualize** All the animals are making sounds at once. What picture do you get in your mind of what is happening behind Miss Fry's door?

On Parents' Night, the mothers and fathers walked around
the classroom with great big smiles on their faces.
"Isn't it great," they said, "that Miss Fry loves pets so?"

Only Roger's cricket sat quietly in his box.

"You must miss your garden," Miss Fry said.

*Chirrup,* said Moe softly. He crawled under one of his shiny green leaves.

chirrup

On the last day of school, Miss Fry's class had
a party with balloons, hats, and ice-cream cups.
"Good-bye, children!" Miss Fry sang out.
"Have a nice summer . . . *and don't forget to*

144

# take home your pets!"

One by one, the children disappeared,
and with them went their pets.

145

"No more pets," said Miss Fry.

She looked around the quiet, empty room.

Then Miss Fry noticed a box sitting on her desk.

She peeked inside.  A little face looked up at her.

It almost seemed to smile.

A note inside read:

DEAR MISS FRY,
PLEASE TAKE
CARE
OF MOE.
HE LIKES YOU
BEST.

ROGER

"How lucky for me," said Miss Fry.

Moe did a huge somersault—up, up in the air.

Miss Fry carried her new pet to her quiet little house and placed him in the garden, among the rainbow of roses.

That night, Miss Fry opened her window.
She climbed into bed. She turned off the lamp.
By the light of the moon, from outside in the
garden, came a happy noise.
*Chirrup-chirrup!*

Welcome home, Moe. What a wonderful pet you are.

# Your Turn

## Animal Parade

**Make a Mask**

Think about the pets that the children in Miss Fry's class brought to school. Which pet do you like best? Make a paper plate mask of that animal. With a small group, take turns telling why you each chose the animal you did. Then have an animal parade with your class. SMALL GROUP

**Turn and Talk** — ## Tell About Setting

Where do most of the events in *Teacher's Pets* take place? With a partner, look at the first page of the story. Find clues about the story's setting, using the picture and words. Talk about what you find. STORY STRUCTURE

Welcome To 2nd Grade

# Social Studies

| | |
|---|---|
| wonderful | share |
| noises | noticed |
| quiet | bursting |
| sprinkled | suddenly |

**GENRE**

**Informational text** gives facts about a topic. This is a pamphlet.

**TEXT FOCUS**

A **map** is a drawing of a town, state, or other place.

# See Westburg by Bus!

## Welcome to Westburg!

The best way to see our town is on Bus Number 33. Get the bus in front of our Welcome Center. After you get on board, read this pamphlet. Just follow the numbers sprinkled on the map as you go.

We are happy to share our wonderful town with you.

SILVER RIVER

Brown Street

Red Street

② LIBRARY

Blue Avenue

Pine Street

① WELCOME CENTER

③ Rainbow Park

**① Welcome Center**

Find the Welcome Center. It is bursting with pamphlets, maps, and books about Westburg.

**② Library**

The Public Library is on Blue Avenue. The children's room is a great place for books, computer games, and movies.

**③ Rainbow Park**

Cross Blue Avenue to get to Westburg's largest park. People come here to play, walk, or have some quiet time.

**Key**

river ▬▬▬     bus route ▬ ▬ ▬     bridge ▤▤

**4** **School**

Take the bridge across the Silver River.  When you get on the other side, Chávez Elementary will be on your left.

**5** **Bike Path**

Have you **noticed** how the bike path follows the curves of the Silver River? What a great view!

**6** **Safety Center**

If you **suddenly** hear siren **noises** as you pass the Safety Center, a fire truck or ambulance may be whizzing by!

# Making Connections

 **Text to Self**

**Write About School** If you were a student in Miss Fry's class, what pet would you bring to school? Write to explain. Share your ideas with a partner.

 **Text to Text**

**Connect to Math** Would you rather spend a day in Miss Fry's room or a day in Westburg? Vote with the children in your class. Record the votes on a chart and find the difference.

| Miss Fry's class | Westburg |
|---|---|
| ‖‖‖ ‖ | ‖‖‖ ‖‖‖‖ |

 **Text to World**

**Research an Animal** Choose a pet from the story *Teacher's Pets* that you would like to know more about. Research how to care for that type of pet.

# Grammar

**Singular and Plural Nouns**  A **singular noun** names one person, animal, place, or thing.  A **plural noun** names more than one person, animal, place, or thing.  Add -s to most nouns to name more than one.

| Sentences with Singular Nouns | Sentences with Plural Nouns |
| --- | --- |
| The teacher talks loudly. | The two teachers talk to their students. |
| This playground looks big. | All playgrounds are fun. |

**Turn and Talk**  **Work with a partner.  Read the sentences aloud.  Name the singular nouns and plural nouns.**

1 Two crickets sat in a cage.

2 My friend has three cats.

3 Her bird ate some seeds.

4 Our teacher loves pets!

**Conventions** Edit your writing carefully. Make sure you have written nouns that name more than one in the correct plural form.

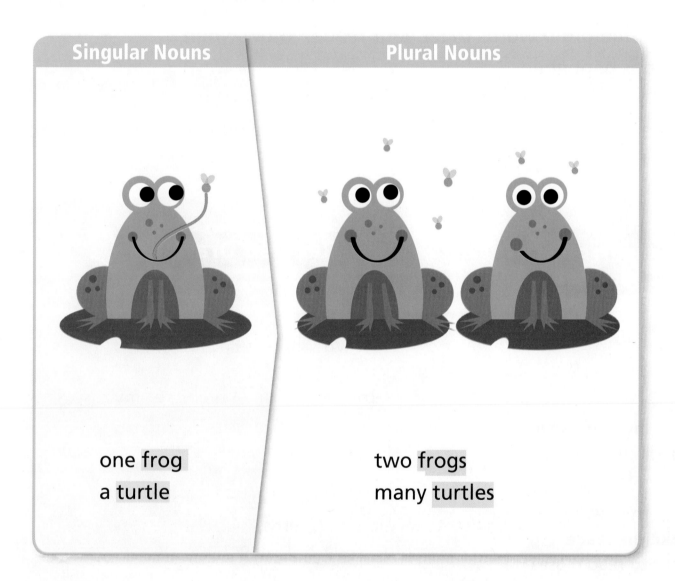

| Singular Nouns | Plural Nouns |
|---|---|
| one frog<br>a turtle | two frogs<br>many turtles |

## Connect Grammar to Writing

**When you edit your true story, be sure to write the correct form of all plural nouns.**

# Write to Narrate

☑ **Sentence Fluency** When you write a **true story**, use time-order words to let your reader know when things happened.

Raj drafted a story about the day he read a story to the class. Later, he added time-order words to tell when things happened.

## Writing Process Checklist

**Prewrite**

**Draft**

▶ **Revise**

☑ Does my story have a beginning, middle, and end?

☑ Does the beginning make the reader want to read more?

☑ Did I use time-order words to tell when things happened?

☑ Does the ending wrap things up?

**Edit**

**Publish and Share**

## Revised Draft

Last week it
~~It~~ was my turn for the

Author's Chair. I chose my

story about Uncle Sanjay

At first
and the spider. I was

Then
nervous. I practiced in

front of my family.

# My Day
# in the Author's Chair
## by Raj Bhatti

Last week it was my turn for the Author's Chair. I chose my story about Uncle Sanjay and the spider. At first I was nervous. Then I practiced in front of my family. Finally I read the story to the class. I read the part about how Uncle Sanjay screamed when he saw the spider. The class laughed.

> I used time-order words to tell when things happened.

## Reading as a Writer

What time-order words does Raj use to tell when things happened? What time-order words can you add to your true story?

157

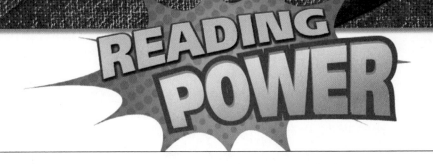
> Read the next two selections. Think about the order of events in each selection.

# A Birthday Surprise

Mom was baking a cake. "It's for Mrs. Lopez's birthday," Mom said. "She is eighty-one years old today." Carlos liked Mrs. Lopez. She had some trouble seeing, but it never slowed her down. He wanted to do something special for her.

Then he got a superb idea. He got a book and went next door. "Surprise, Mrs. Lopez!" he said. "I'm going to read to you."

"I love to listen to you read," she said.

# The King's Woods

Long ago, an old man lived deep in the king's woods. One day the prince rode through the woods. He saw the old man and shouted, "Get out of the king's woods!"

The man went to pack his things. Then he saw a sad sight. The prince's horse had fallen. The prince was injured. The old man ran to get help.

When the prince was better, he called for the old man. "You saved my life," he said. "You may have anything you want."

"I only want to stay in the woods," the man replied. So he did.

# Unit 1 Wrap-Up

## The Big Idea

**Good Neighbors** Draw a picture of a friend in your neighborhood. Then write some sentences about what you like about the person. Cut out the sentences and glue them under the picture.

This is Maria Lopez. She jumps rope with me every day.

## Listening and Speaking

**Who Am I?** In a small group, play a guessing game about community helpers. Take turns acting out community jobs, such as fire fighter, school teacher, or crossing guard. Ask the group to guess each job.

# Nature Watch

# Unit 2

# Big Idea

Nature can
teach us
many things.

# Paired Selections

**TARGET VOCABULARY**

**shaped**

**branches**

**pond**

**beaks**

**deepest**

**break**

**hang**

**winding**

Vocabulary
Reader

Context
Cards

# Vocabulary in Context

- Read each **Context Card**.

- Use a Vocabulary word to tell about something you did.

**1** **shaped**

Have you ever seen a home shaped like this? It is curved like a ball.

**2** **branches**

Tree branches high above the ground are a good home for a sloth.

### 3 pond

Turtles make their home in a pond, or small lake.

### 4 beaks

These birds use their beaks to build their home.

### 5 deepest

The deepest part of the ocean is this eel's home.

### 6 break

This home won't break! It is made of strong rock.

### 7 hang

These bats hang upside down in their cave.

### 8 winding

Some animal homes have long, winding tunnels that twist and turn.

163

# Background

**Animal Homes** Some birds build their homes with their beaks. Some insects build nests shaped like balls. They hang from branches. Often bats live in the deepest parts of caves. A frog may live by a pond. A clam lives in a shell that other animals cannot break easily. A groundhog digs a burrow that has winding tunnels. No matter where it lives, an animal feels safe in its home.

**Hornet ▶**
Hornets build nests
in tree branches.

**◀ Honey Bee**
Honey bees live in hives. Inside
the hives bees store honey.

# Comprehension

**Text and Graphic Features**

The author chose the title, *Animals Building Homes*, to tell you the topic, or what the book is about. She also chose words, headings, and photos to make her ideas clear. Use a chart like this to list some features. Then tell why you think the author used them.

| Text or Graphic Feature | Page Number | Purpose |
|---|---|---|
|  |  |  |

✔ TARGET STRATEGY  **Question**

Think of the questions you have about how animals build their homes. Then look for some answers by reading the text and studying the graphic features in the article.

## TARGET VOCABULARY

| | |
|---|---|
| shaped | deepest |
| branches | break |
| pond | hang |
| beaks | winding |

## TARGET SKILL

**Text and Graphic Features** Tell how words go with photos.

| | | |
|---|---|---|
| | | |

## TARGET STRATEGY

**Question** Ask questions about what you are reading.

**GENRE**
**Informational Text** gives facts about a topic.

**MEET THE AUTHOR**

# Wendy Perkins

Can you guess why Wendy Perkins has been called a "walking animal encyclopedia"? It's because her mind is filled with facts and information about all kinds of animals.

Ms. Perkins has written nonfiction books about animal eyes, ears, feet, feathers, noses, teeth, and tails. She also writes articles for *Highlights for Children* and a magazine put out by the San Diego Zoo called *Zoonooz*.

# Animals Building Homes

by Wendy Perkins

## Essential Question

How can chapter headings help you?

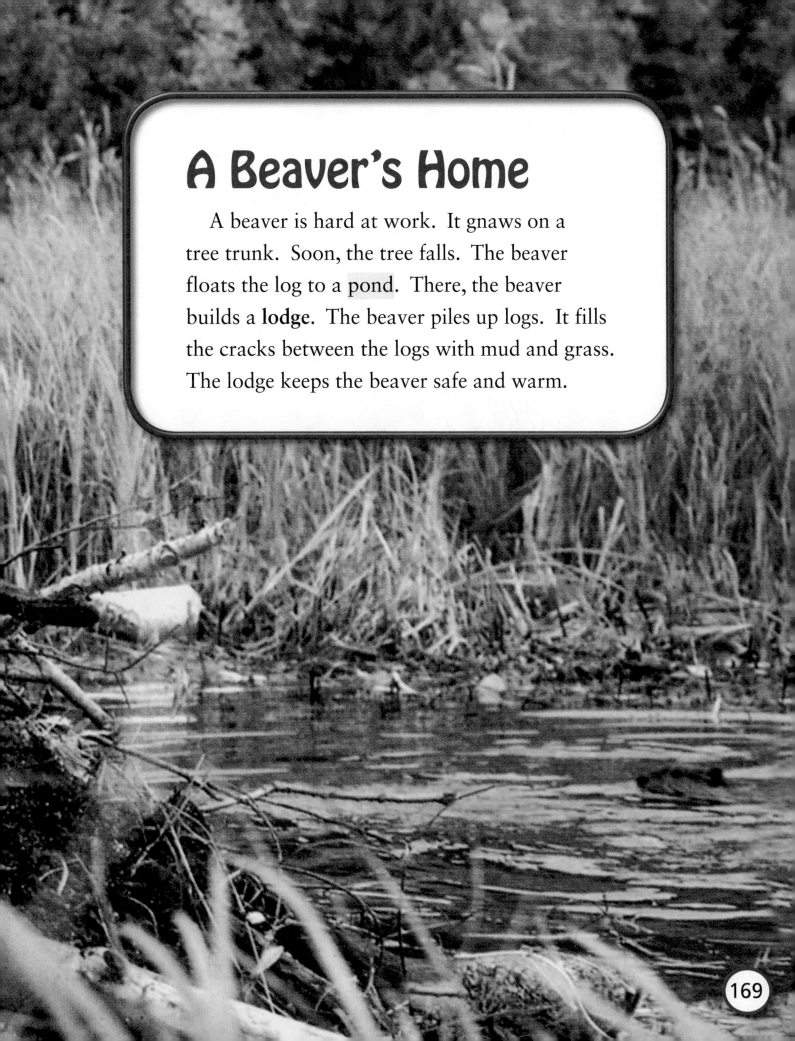

# A Beaver's Home

A beaver is hard at work. It gnaws on a tree trunk. Soon, the tree falls. The beaver floats the log to a pond. There, the beaver builds a **lodge**. The beaver piles up logs. It fills the cracks between the logs with mud and grass. The lodge keeps the beaver safe and warm.

# Safe at Home

Most animals need a home. Homes keep animals safe from **predators**, rain, snow, or the hot sun. Some animals live in their homes for life. Other animals live in their homes long enough to raise their **offspring** or **survive** hot or cold weather.

✔ STOP AND THINK
**Text and Graphic Features**
Why are some of the words in dark print?

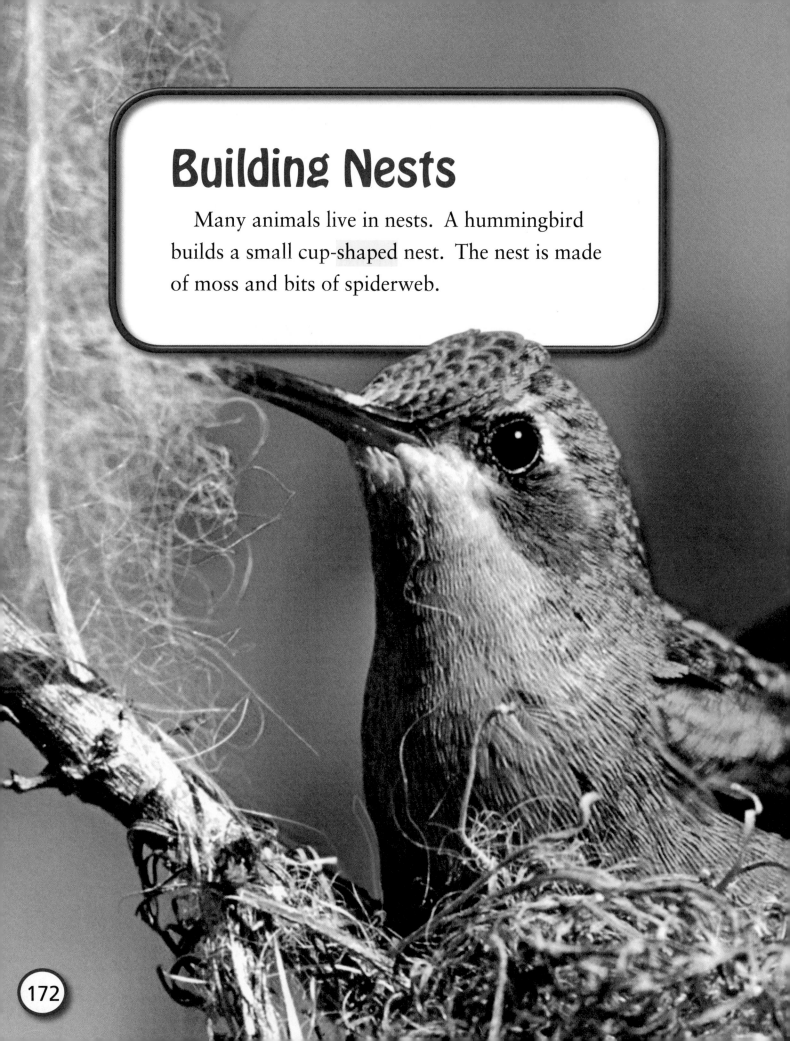

# Building Nests

Many animals live in nests. A hummingbird builds a small cup-shaped nest. The nest is made of moss and bits of spiderweb.

A mouse makes a grass nest in the shape of a ball. The mouse hides its nest in tall grass or in a tunnel under the ground.

# Careful Builders

Some animals put a lot of work into building their homes. Weaver birds make nests that hang from tree branches. The birds carefully weave grass and leaves together. Weaver birds use their feet and beaks to tie knots in the grass.

# Working Together

Animals can work together to build homes. Termites build **mounds** made out of mud mixed with **saliva**. Other animals cannot easily break through the hard mud.

**STOP AND THINK**
**Question** What question about how termites work together does this page answer?

Polyps are animals that make coral reefs. A polyp builds a **limestone** cup around its body for protection. The cups of the polyps grow together to make a coral reef.

# Making a Burrow

**Burrows** are holes in the ground where some animals live. Gophers use their teeth and paws to dig long, winding tunnels. They make rooms in the deepest parts of the tunnels. The gophers hide their offspring and food in these rooms.

# Home Improvement

Some animals live in homes made by other animals. Chickadees use tree holes made by woodpeckers. Chickadees bring grass and moss into the hole. They build a nest for their chicks.

**STOP AND THINK**
**Author's Craft** Why does the author name this page "Home Improvement"?

179

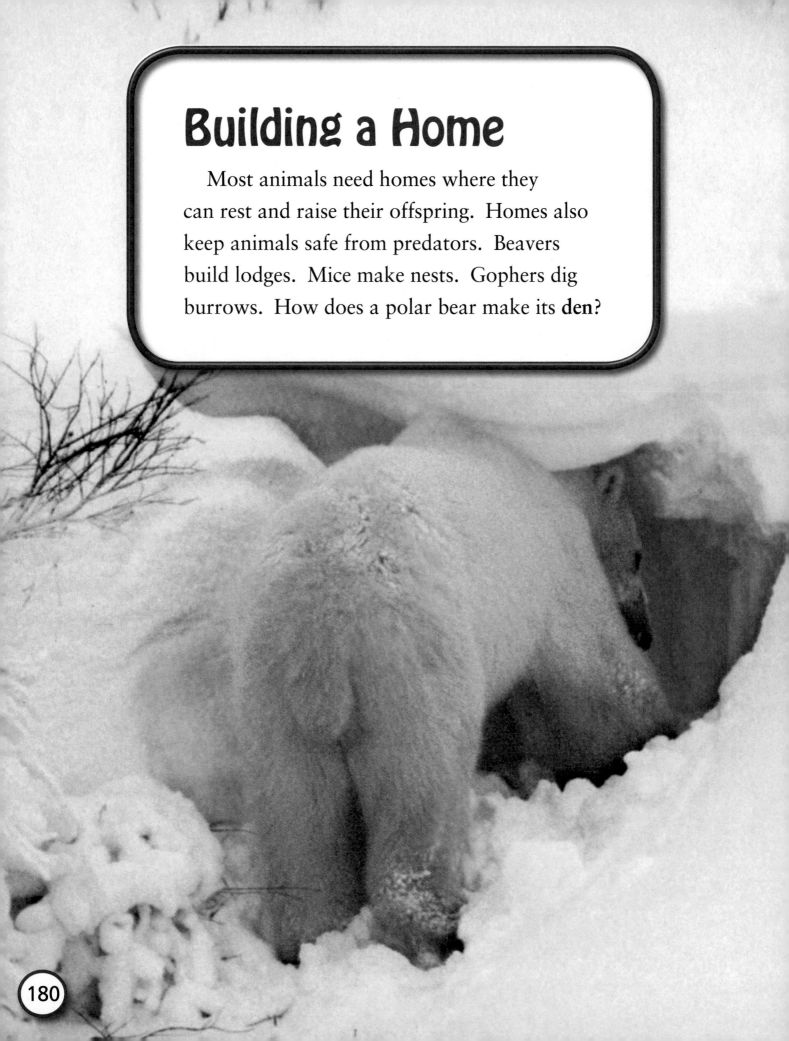

# Building a Home

Most animals need homes where they can rest and raise their offspring. Homes also keep animals safe from predators. Beavers build lodges. Mice make nests. Gophers dig burrows. How does a polar bear make its **den**?

# Your Turn

## Favorite Animal Homes

**Write to Describe**

What wild animal do you want to learn about? Use books and other sources to find out about the animal you chose. Write a few sentences that describe the animal's home. Share your work with classmates. SCIENCE

## Turn and Talk — Hunt for Headings

Look back through *Animals Building Homes.* How did the headings help you understand what you read? How would the book be different with no headings? Work with a partner to answer these questions. TEXT AND GRAPHIC FEATURES

# Hiding at the Pond

**by Sue LaBella**

**Cast of Characters**

Bullfrog

Snapping Turtle

Walking Stick

**Bullfrog:** (jumping) What a great day to jump! I'll hop along this winding path around the pond.

**Walking Stick:** Watch out for the snapping turtle.

**Bullfrog:** (stops and looks around) Who said that?

**Walking Stick:** I did.

**Bullfrog:** (looking around) I can't see you.

**Walking Stick:** Look closely at the tree branches. I'll hang down and wiggle.

**Bullfrog:** You look like a stick!

**Walking Stick:** That's right. I'm a bug called a walking stick. I have a stick-shaped body. It's great camouflage. Birds think I'm a twig, so they don't grab me with their beaks.

**Bullfrog:** My brown and green colors help me hide in the grass and in the pond.

**Snapping Turtle:** But not on the path!

**Bullfrog:** (surprised) Your dark color hides you well.

**Snapping Turtle:** I know. It hides me in the mud and in the deepest part of the pond, too.

**Bullfrog:** Your jaws look strong. Can they break things in half?

**Snapping Turtle:** Yes.

**Bullfrog:** (jumping away) Yikes! Bye!

# Making Connections

## Text to Self

**Share Experiences** Think about the animal homes in *Animals Building Homes*. Which have you seen before? Share your ideas with a partner.

## Text to Text

**Explore Homes at Ponds** Work with a team to list animals from each selection that live in or near a pond. Discuss how these animals are alike and different. Name books and other sources you might use to find more information.

## Text to World

**Connect to Science** What else would your class like to learn about animal homes? Choose one topic to research as a group.

# Grammar

**More Plural Nouns** A **plural noun** names more than one person, animal, place, or thing. Add *-s* to most nouns to name more than one. Add *-es* to nouns that end with *s*, *x*, *ch*, and *sh*.

| Singular Nouns | Plural Nouns |
|---|---|
| one fox | two foxes |
| the class | many classes |
| a finch | some finches |
| the dish | three dishes |

 **Read each sentence. Write the plural of each underlined noun.**

❶ The <u>boss</u> was angry.

❷ The beaver used a <u>bunch</u> of wood.

❸ This <u>bush</u> is heavy!

❹ The squirrel hid in a <u>box</u>.

**Sentence Fluency** You may join two short sentences with the same predicate to make one longer sentence. Write **and** between the two subjects. Your writing will be smoother.

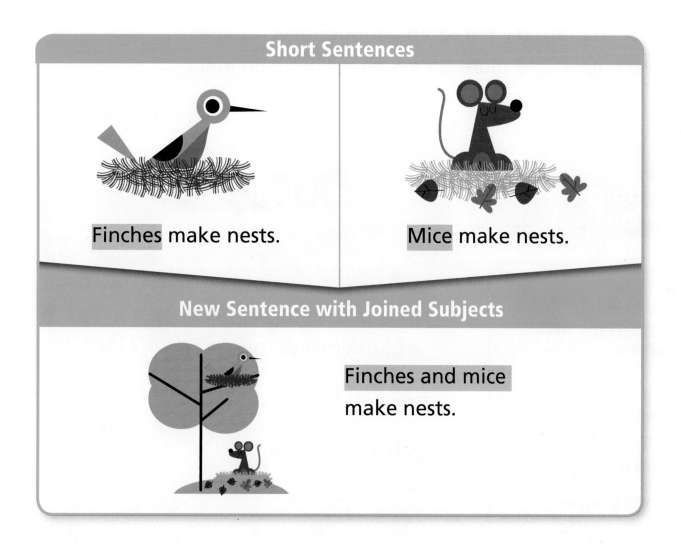

**Short Sentences**

Finches make nests.

Mice make nests.

**New Sentence with Joined Subjects**

Finches and mice make nests.

## Connect Grammar to Writing

**When you revise your writing, try joining two short sentences that have the same predicate.**

# Write to Inform

**✓ Ideas** When you write an **informational paragraph**, make sure you include details that tell about the main idea.

Sean drafted a paragraph about beaver homes. Later, he added more details about his main idea.

**✓ Ideas**

Do all my details support the main idea?

**✓ Organization**

Does my topic sentence tell the main idea?

**✓ Word Choice**

Did I use exact words?

**✓ Conventions**

Did I write neatly and leave margins?

## Revised Draft

They use parts of trees to build their homes there. Beavers live on ponds. ∧A

beaver can use its teeth to

Then the tree falls.

gnaw on a tree.∧

# Beaver Lodges

by Sean McDonald

Beavers live on ponds. They use parts of trees to build their homes there. A beaver can use its teeth to gnaw on a tree. Then the tree falls. Beavers float logs to a place to build a lodge. The beaver uses mud and grass to fill cracks. That makes the lodge warm.

I added more details about beavers' homes.

## Reading as a Writer

Which details did Sean add to tell more about his main idea? Where can you add details to your own paragraph?

**blooming**

**shovels**

**scent**

**tough**

**wrinkled**

**plain**

**muscles**

**nodded**

Vocabulary
Reader

Context
Cards

# Vocabulary in Context

- Read each **Context Card**.

- Make up a new sentence that uses a Vocabulary word.

### 1 blooming

Sunflowers are blooming in the field. They face the sun as their flowers grow.

### 2 shovels

These children use shovels to help plant a tree.

### 3 scent

Roses have a scent, or smell, that is as sweet as perfume.

### 4 tough

A pumpkin has a tough outer skin that is hard to break.

### 5 wrinkled

A raisin is a dried, wrinkled grape, but it is still sweet.

### 6 plain

The plant on the left is plain. The plant on the right is fancy.

### 7 muscles

It takes strong muscles to use a loaded wheelbarrow.

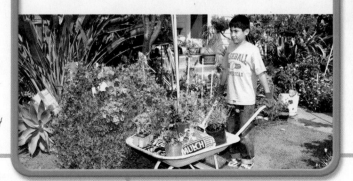

### 8 nodded

The girl nodded her head up and down to show that she would help in the garden.

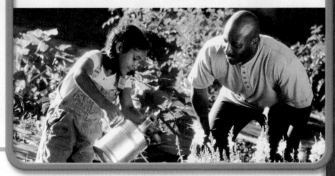

# Background

**Growing a Garden** A flower garden has blooming flowers. Their scent fills the air. A vegetable garden looks plain, but it has plants to eat. Gardens take work. Gardeners need strong muscles to turn the soil with shovels. They plant seeds, and soon wrinkled sprouts unfold. When tough weeds grow, gardeners pull them up. If you have ever asked if gardening is hard work, the gardener will surely have nodded yes!

The flowers in this garden needed a lot of water to grow.

# Comprehension

**✔ TARGET SKILL** **Conclusions**

As you read *The Ugly Vegetables*, use story clues to figure out more about the events and characters. Use clues to draw conclusions, or make smart guesses, about what the author does not say. Write the clues you use and a conclusion in a chart like this.

**✔ TARGET STRATEGY** **Analyze/Evaluate**

As you read, think carefully. Do your conclusions help you understand the story? Do you learn more about gardening? Use your conclusions to decide how you feel about *The Ugly Vegetables*.

*The*
**Ugly Vegetables**
*by Grace Lin*

✔ **TARGET VOCABULARY**

| | |
|---|---|
| blooming | wrinkled |
| shovels | plain |
| scent | muscles |
| tough | nodded |

✔ **TARGET SKILL**

**Conclusions** Use details to figure out more about the text.

✔ **TARGET STRATEGY**

**Analyze/Evaluate** Tell how you feel about the text, and why.

**GENRE**

**Realistic fiction** is a story that could happen in real life.

**MEET THE AUTHOR AND ILLUSTRATOR**

# Grace Lin

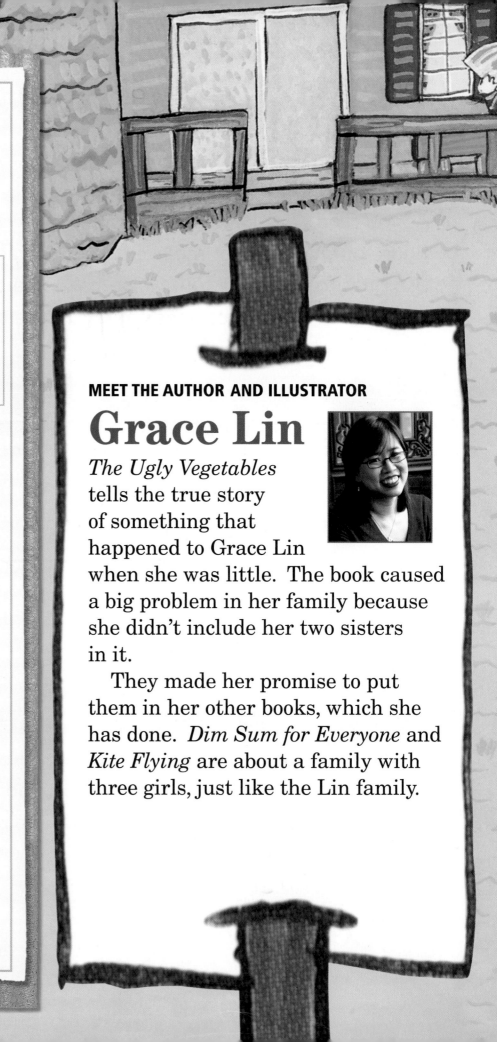

*The Ugly Vegetables* tells the true story of something that happened to Grace Lin when she was little. The book caused a big problem in her family because she didn't include her two sisters in it.

They made her promise to put them in her other books, which she has done. *Dim Sum for Everyone* and *Kite Flying* are about a family with three girls, just like the Lin family.

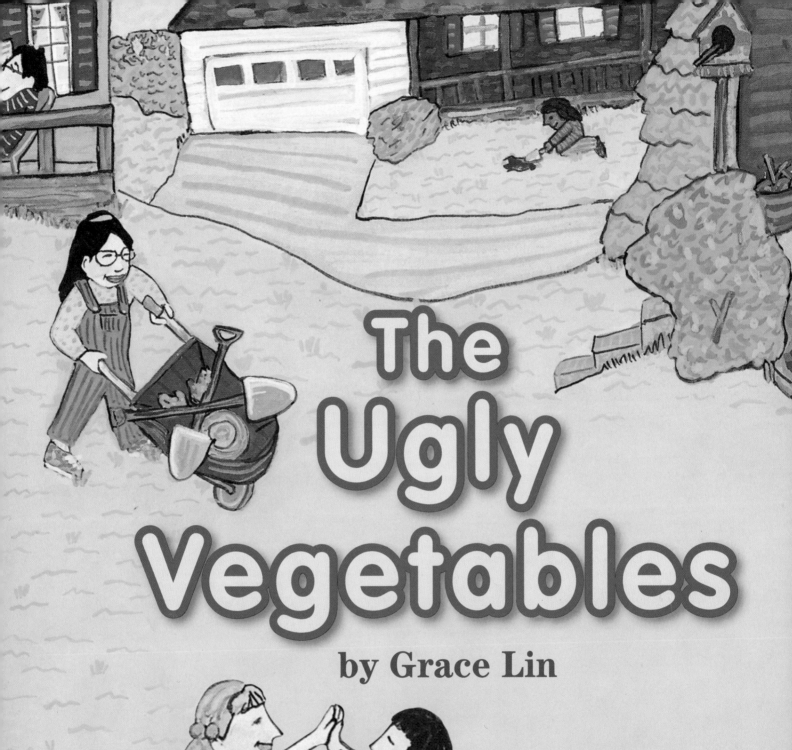

# The Ugly Vegetables

## by Grace Lin

**Essential Question**

What helps you make decisions about a character?

195

In the spring I helped my mother start our garden. We used tall shovels to turn the grass upside down, and I saw pink worms wriggle around. It was hard work. When we stopped to rest, we saw that the neighbors were starting their gardens too.

"Hello, Irma!" my mother called to Mrs. Crumerine. Mrs. Crumerine was digging too. She was using a small shovel, one that fit in her hand.

"Mommy," I asked, "why are we using such big shovels? Mrs. Crumerine has a small one."

"Because our garden needs more digging," she said.

I helped my mother plant the seeds, and we dragged the hose to the garden.

"Hi, Linda! Hi, Mickey!" I called to the Fitzgeralds. They were sprinkling water on their garden with green watering cans.

"Mommy," I asked, "why are we using a hose? Linda and Mickey use watering cans."

"Because our garden needs more water," she said.

 **STOP AND THINK**
**Conclusions** What can you tell about the people in this neighborhood? Explain your answer.

Then my mother drew funny pictures on pieces of paper, and I stuck them into the garden.

"Hello, Roseanne!" my mother called across the street to Mrs. Angelhowe.

"Mommy," I asked, "why are we sticking these papers in the garden?  Mrs. Angelhowe has seed packages in her garden."

"Because our garden is going to grow Chinese vegetables," she told me.  "These are the names of the vegetables in Chinese, so I can tell which plants are growing where."

One day I saw our garden growing. Little green
stems that looked like grass had popped out from the
ground.

"Our garden's growing!" I yelled. "Our garden's
growing!"

I rushed over to the neighbors' gardens to see if theirs
had grown. Their plants looked like little leaves.

"Mommy," I asked, "why do our plants look like
grass? The neighbors' plants look different."

"Because they are growing flowers," she said.

"Why can't we grow flowers?" I asked.

"These are better than flowers," she said.

Soon all the neighbors' gardens were blooming. Up
and down the street grew rainbows of flowers.

The wind always smelled sweet, and butterflies and
bees flew everywhere. Everyone's garden was beautiful,
except for ours.

Ours was all dark green and ugly.

"Why didn't we grow flowers?" I asked again.

"These are better than flowers," Mommy said again.

I looked, but saw only black-purple-green vines, fuzzy wrinkled leaves, prickly stems, and a few little yellow flowers.

"I don't think so," I said.

"You wait and see," Mommy said.

Before long, our vegetables grew. Some were big and lumpy. Some were thin and green and covered with bumps. Some were just plain icky yellow. They were ugly vegetables.

Sometimes I would go over to the neighbors' and look at their pretty gardens. They would show the poppies and peonies and petunias to me, and I would feel sad that our garden wasn't as nice.

One day my mother and I picked the vegetables from
the garden.  We filled a whole wheelbarrow full of them.
We wheeled them to the kitchen.  My mother washed
them and took a big knife and started to chop them.

"Aie-yow!" she said when she cut them.  She had to
use all her muscles.  The vegetables were hard and tough.

"This is sheau hwang gua (show hwang gwa),"
Mommy said, handing me a bumpy, curled vegetable.  She
pointed at the other vegetables.  "This is shiann tsay
(shen zai).  That's a torng hau (tung how)."

I went outside to play. While I was playing catch with Mickey, a magical aroma filled the air. I saw the neighbors standing on their porches with their eyes closed, smelling the sky. They took deep breaths of air, like they were trying to eat the smell.

The wind carried it up and down the street.  Even
the bees and the butterflies seemed to smell the scent
in the breeze.

I smelled it too. It made me hungry, and it was
coming from my house!

When I followed it to my house, my mother was putting a big bowl of soup on the table. The soup was yellow and red and green and pink.

"This is a special soup," Mommy said, and she smiled.

She gave me a small bowl full of it and I tasted it. It was so good! The flavors of the soup seemed to dance in my mouth and laugh all the way down to my stomach. I smiled.

"Do you like it?" Mommy asked me.

I nodded and held out my bowl for some more.

"It's made from our vegetables," she told me.

**STOP AND THINK**
**Author's Craft** What does the author write that tells how good the soup tastes?

Then the doorbell rang, and we ran to open the door.

All our neighbors were standing at the door holding flowers.

"We noticed you were cooking." Mr. Fitzgerald laughed as he held out his flowers. "And we thought maybe you might be interested in a trade!"

**STOP AND THINK**
**Analyze/Evaluate** Would this neighborhood be a good place to live? Use details to tell why.

We laughed too, and my mother gave them each their own bowl of her special soup.

My mother told them what each vegetable was and how she grew it. She gave them the soup recipe and put some soup into jars for them to take home. I ate five bowls of soup.

It was the best dinner ever.

The next spring, when my mother was starting her garden, we planted some flowers next to the Chinese vegetables. Mrs. Crumerine, the Fitzgeralds, and the Angelhowes planted some Chinese vegetables next to their flowers.

Soon the whole neighborhood was growing Chinese vegetables in their gardens. Up and down the street, little green plants poked out of the ground. Some looked like leaves and some looked like grass, and when the flowers started blooming, you could smell soup in the air.

## Your Turn

### Vegetable Fun

**Plan a Meal**

The mother in *The Ugly Vegetables* makes a tasty soup from vegetables she grew in her garden. Name a vegetable you like. Talk with classmates about which ones they like, too. Plan a meal that uses all your favorites.

SMALL GROUP

### Turn and Talk — Super Soup

Why did the girl say her soup dinner was "the best ever"? Work with a partner to answer the question. Use story clues in your answer. CONCLUSIONS

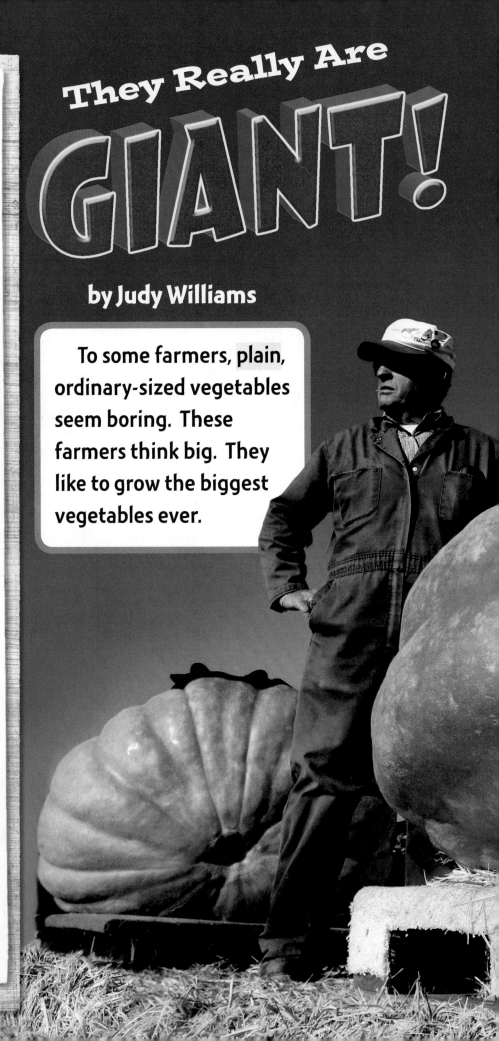

# They Really Are GIANT!

by Judy Williams

To some farmers, plain, ordinary-sized vegetables seem boring. These farmers think big. They like to grow the biggest vegetables ever.

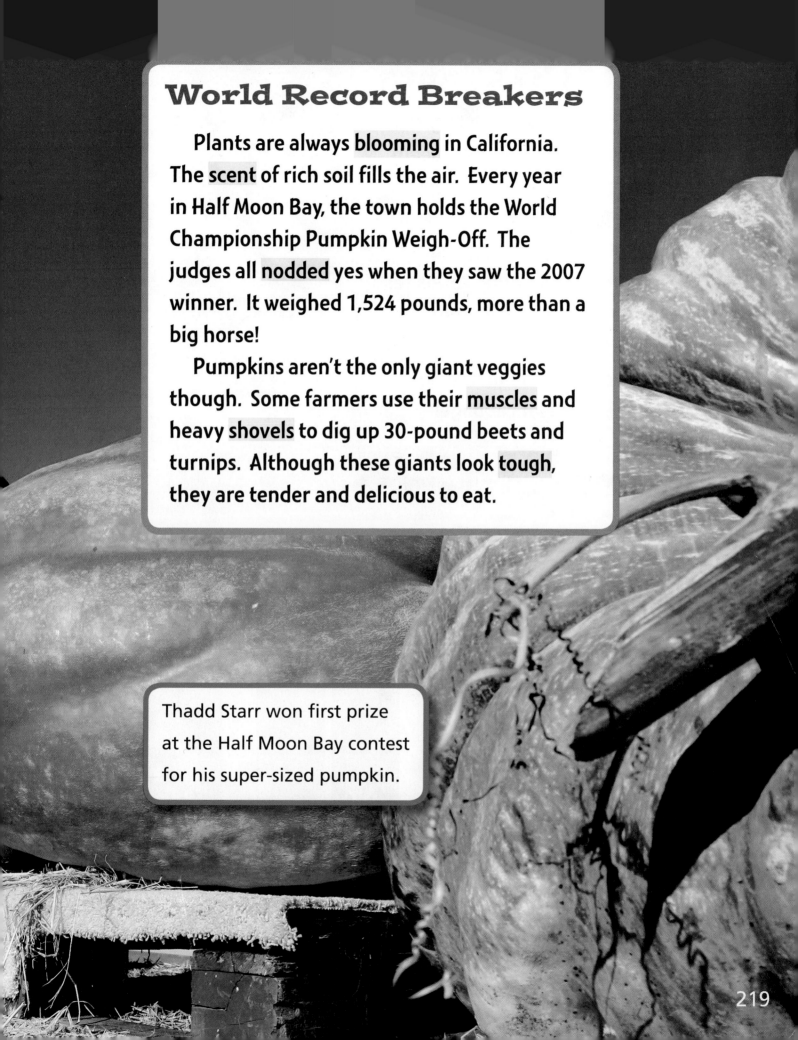

# World Record Breakers

Plants are always blooming in California. The scent of rich soil fills the air. Every year in Half Moon Bay, the town holds the World Championship Pumpkin Weigh-Off. The judges all nodded yes when they saw the 2007 winner. It weighed 1,524 pounds, more than a big horse!

Pumpkins aren't the only giant veggies though. Some farmers use their muscles and heavy shovels to dig up 30-pound beets and turnips. Although these giants look tough, they are tender and delicious to eat.

Thadd Starr won first prize at the Half Moon Bay contest for his super-sized pumpkin.

# Home of the Giants

Alaska might be the home of giant veggies. More giant vegetables seem to grow there than any other place in the world. Long summer days and good soil make veggies grow and grow. You can see 98-pound cabbages at the Alaska State Fair in Palmer.

Seven-year-old Brenna Dinkel from Wasilla, Alaska, looks small next to this giant wrinkled leaf cabbage!

## How Big Are They?

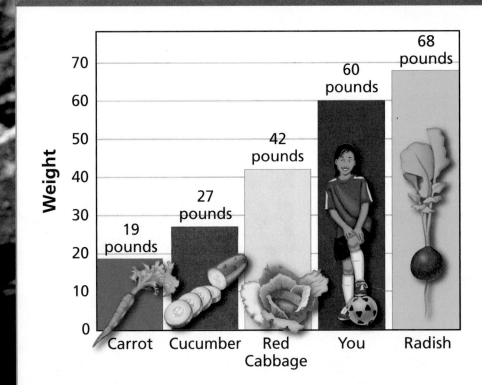

Weight

- Carrot: 19 pounds
- Cucumber: 27 pounds
- Red Cabbage: 42 pounds
- You: 60 pounds
- Radish: 68 pounds

# Making Connections

 **Text to Self**

**Make a List** List the steps that the characters take to plant and care for their vegetables in *The Ugly Vegetables*. Which step do you think is the most fun?

 **Text to Text**

**Compare Vegetables** Would you rather grow ugly vegetables like those in *The Ugly Vegetables* or giant ones like those in "They Really Are Giant!"? Explain.

 **Text to World**

**Connect to Social Studies** In *The Ugly Vegetables*, Mommy says she is growing Chinese vegetables. Find China on a map or globe. Talk with a partner about what you found. Listen carefully to what your partner says.

# Grammar

**Proper Nouns  Proper nouns** are the special names of people, animals, places, or things.  Proper nouns begin with **capital letters**.

| Nouns | Proper Nouns |
|---|---|
| neighbor | Roseanne Smith |
| pet | Fluffy |
| road | Main Street |
| state | Texas |
| country | China |

**Try This!**  **Write each sentence correctly. Remember to begin the proper nouns with capital letters.**

1. There are many gardens in centerville.

2. My friend molly bowen picked apples.

3. Our dog spot is digging up the roses!

222

**Word Choice** A proper noun names a special person, animal, place, or thing. A proper noun is one kind of exact noun. Use exact nouns in your writing to paint a picture in your reader's mind.

| Nouns | Exact Nouns |
|---|---|
| The man has a garden on a street. | Mr. Carter has a garden on Oak Street. |

## Connect Grammar to Writing

**When you revise your summary paragraph, look for nouns you can change to more exact nouns.**

# Write to Inform

**✓ Organization** A **summary** tells what happens in a story. It puts the events in the same order.

Kayla drafted a summary of the first part of *The Ugly Vegetables*. Later, she put the events in the right order.

## Revised Draft

A girl helps her mother start a garden. The girl keeps seeing things they're doing differently from their neighbors. To water the garden, she and her mother use a hose. The neighbors use watering cans. The neighbors are using smaller shovels.

# My Summary

by Kayla Higgs

A girl helps her mother start a garden. The girl keeps seeing things they're doing differently from their neighbors. The neighbors are using smaller shovels. To water the garden, she and her mother use a hose. The neighbors use watering cans. She and her mother stick pictures in their garden. The girl asks why their garden is different from the neighbors' flower gardens. Her mother says the vegetables they are growing are better than flowers.

> I moved sentences around to tell things in the order in which they happened.

## Reading as a Writer

Why did Kayla move sentences? What can you move in your writing to put events in the right order?

**TARGET VOCABULARY**

**beware**

**damage**

**bend**

**flash**

**pounding**

**prevent**

**reach**

**equal**

Vocabulary
Reader

Context
Cards

# Vocabulary in Context

- Read each **Context Card**.

- Talk about a picture. Use a different Vocabulary word from the one on the card.

**1**
### beware
Beware of dangerous weather when a storm siren sounds its warning.

**2**
### damage
Hail and strong winds can do a lot of harm. They can damage crops.

**3  bend**

High winds have caused the trunks of these trees to bend, or curve.

**4  flash**

The flash of lightning bolts lit up the dark night sky.

**5  pounding**

Pounding waves hit the beach hard in a storm.

**6  prevent**

Heavy snow may prevent, or stop, cars and trucks from traveling.

**7  reach**

In a flood, water can reach, or go as high as, rooftops.

**8  equal**

The height of the snow is equal to three feet.

# Background

✔ **TARGET VOCABULARY** **Storm Warning** Beware!
A flash of lightning or a boom of thunder means a storm is coming. Strong winds that bend big trees are another sign of a storm. Pounding hailstones can damage homes and cars. One way to prevent getting hurt in a storm is to pay attention to the sky. Clouds shaped like a funnel equal a tornado. You need to find a safe place before the storm can reach where you are.

This chart shows how scientists indicate the strength of a tornado.

# Comprehension

**Main Ideas and Details**

Use the title to help you figure out the topic of
*Super Storms*. Then, as you read, think about the
main, or important, ideas about the different
storms. Use a web like this to note details that tell
about each main idea.

✔ TARGET STRATEGY **Visualize**

Use details about each main idea to help you visualize,
or form a picture of, what the author is describing. The
pictures you form will help you remember main ideas
about different kinds of storms.

### TARGET VOCABULARY

| | |
|---|---|
| beware | pounding |
| damage | prevent |
| bend | reach |
| flash | equal |

### TARGET SKILL

**Main Ideas and Details** Tell important ideas and details about a topic.

### TARGET STRATEGY

**Visualize** Picture what is happening as you read.

**GENRE**
**Informational text** gives facts about a topic.

MEET THE AUTHOR

# SEYMOUR SIMON

As a former science teacher, Seymour Simon loves to visit classrooms and talk with students. Those visits sometimes help him decide what to write about next.

Mr. Simon has written about everything from bats, bears, and bugs to snakes, sharks, and spiders. Of the more than 200 books he has written, *The Paper Airplane Book* is one of his favorites.

# SUPER STORMS

## by Seymour Simon

### Essential Question

How do you know what a story is mostly about?

231

The air around us is always moving and changing. We call these changes weather. Storms are sudden, violent changes in weather.

Every second, hundreds of thunderstorms
are born around the world. Thunderstorms are
heavy rain showers. They can drop millions of
gallons of water in just one minute.

During a thunderstorm, lightning bolts can shoot between clouds and the ground. Lightning can destroy a tree or a small house. It can also start fires in forests and grasslands.

Thunder is the sound lightning makes as it suddenly heats the air. You can tell how far away lightning is. Count the seconds between the flash of light and the sound of thunder. Five seconds equal one mile.

Hailstones are chunks of ice that are tossed up and down by the winds of some thunderstorms. Hail can be the size of a marble or larger than a baseball. Nearly 5,000 hailstorms strike the United States every year. They can destroy crops and damage buildings and cars.

Thunderstorms sometimes give birth to tornadoes. Inside a storm, a funnel-shaped cloud reaches downward. Winds inside a tornado can spin faster than 300 miles per hour. These winds can lift cars off the ground and rip houses apart.

**STOP AND THINK**
**Main Ideas and Details** What is the main idea of this paragraph?

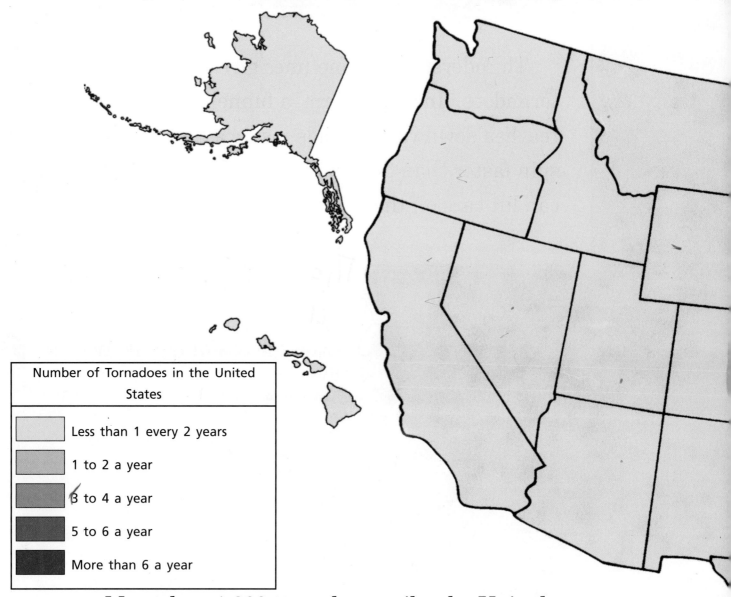

**Number of Tornadoes in the United States**

| | |
|---|---|
| ▢ | Less than 1 every 2 years |
| ▢ | 1 to 2 a year |
| ▢ | 3 to 4 a year |
| ▢ | 5 to 6 a year |
| ▢ | More than 6 a year |

More than 1,000 tornadoes strike the United States each year. Most of them form during spring and summer.

Television and radio stations often give early alerts. A tornado watch means that one may strike during the next few hours. A warning means a tornado has been seen by people or on radar. During a tornado warning you should find shelter in a basement or closet.

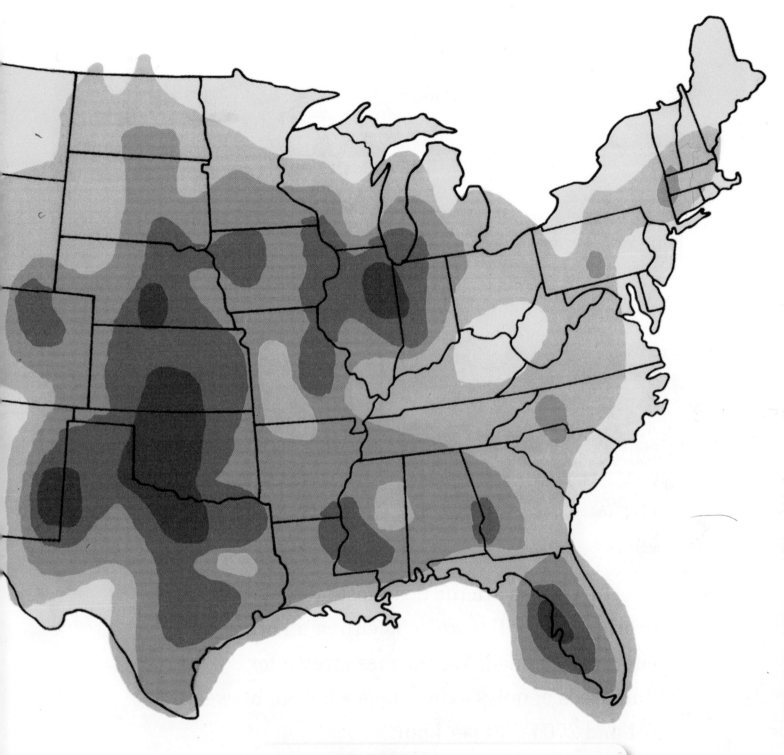

**STOP AND THINK**

**Visualize** How do the colors on the map show where the greatest and the least danger is from tornadoes?

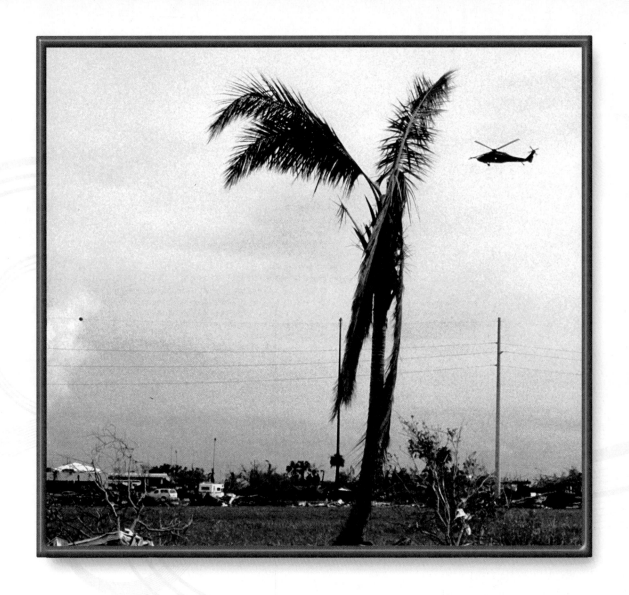

Hurricanes are the deadliest storms in the world. They kill more people than all other storms combined. Hurricanes stretch for hundreds of miles. They have winds of between 74 and 200 miles per hour.

The eye of a hurricane is the quiet center of the storm. Inside the eye, the wind stops blowing, the sun shines, and the sky is blue. But beware, the storm is not over yet.

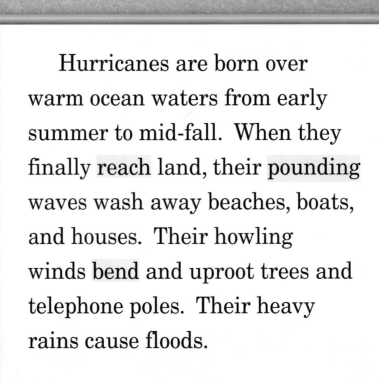

Hurricanes are born over warm ocean waters from early summer to mid-fall. When they finally reach land, their pounding waves wash away beaches, boats, and houses. Their howling winds bend and uproot trees and telephone poles. Their heavy rains cause floods.

**STOP AND THINK**
**Author's Craft** How does the author's description of hurricanes help you visualize these storms?

Blizzards are huge snowstorms. They have winds of at least 35 miles per hour. Usually at least two inches of snow falls per hour. Temperatures are at 20 degrees or lower. Falling and blowing snow make it hard to see in a blizzard.

No one can prevent storms.  But weather reports can predict and warn us when a storm may hit.  The more prepared we are, the safer we will be when the next one strikes.

# Your Turn

## Storm Safety

**Make a Poster**

Bad storms can hurt people, but there are ways to stay safe. Work with your group to make a poster. List two or three ways to stay safe in a storm. Draw or cut out pictures to add to your poster. SMALL GROUP

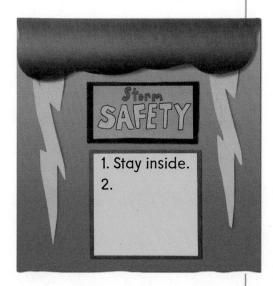

## Turn and Talk — Which Is Which?

With a partner, look back at the first page of *Super Storms.* Which sentences tell about the main idea? Which tell about details? Talk about what you find.

MAIN IDEAS AND DETAILS

✔ **TARGET VOCABULARY**

| | |
|---|---|
| beware | pounding |
| damage | prevent |
| bend | reach |
| flash | equal |

**GENRE**

**Poetry** uses the sound of words to show pictures and feelings.

**TEXT FOCUS**

**Repetition** is the same words used more than once.

# Weather Poems

Many poets write poems about the weather. They might write about a flash of lightning or the way winds bend flowers.

The three poems you will read next are about the weather. Listen to the words that repeat in the poem "Night Drumming for Rain." Does it remind you of pounding raindrops?

## Night Drumming
# for Rain

hi-iya nai-ho-o
earth rumbling
earth rumbling
our basket drum sounding
earth rumbling
everywhere humming
everywhere raining

*Pima*

# Rain

Windy winter rain . . .
   my silly big
   umbrella
tries walking backward

*by Shisei-Jo*
*Translated from Japanese*
*by Peter Beilenson*

# Morning Sun

warming up
my bed
in the morning

the Sun
calls me
through the window

"wake up
get up
come on out"

by Francisco X. Alarcón

# Write a Weather Poem

Write your own weather poem. You might
describe how hot, sunny days equal summer fun.
You might warn friends to beware of a storm
that is about to reach them or damage a special
place. You might even write a funny poem on
how to prevent a storm!

# Making Connections

 **Text to Self**

**Make a Plan** Choose one type of storm from *Super Storms*. With the class, discuss what you would do to stay safe in that kind of weather. Speak only when it is your turn.

 **Text to Text**

**Connect to Science** Think about the weather in *Super Storms* and "Weather Poems." Draw pictures of the two you found most interesting. Write a caption for each picture.

Tornadoes have strong winds that twirl.

 **Text to World**

**Observe Local Weather** What kinds of weather do you get where you live? List each type. Compare your list with a partner's.

# Grammar

**What Is a Verb?** A **verb** names an action that someone or something does or did. A verb is found in the action part, or **predicate**, of a sentence.

---

### Verbs in Sentences

Rain falls.

Strong winds blow.

The storm destroyed homes.

The tornado bent many trees.

---

 **Work with a partner. Read the sentences aloud. Name the verb in each sentence.**

1 I learned about storms.

2 We stay indoors.

3 Tornadoes form in summer.

4 The thunder scared my cat.

**Word Choice** When you write, use exact verbs. They make your sentences come alive and tell your reader exactly what is happening.

| Verb | Exact Verb |
|---|---|
| The hail touched the roof. | The hail pounded the roof. |
| The hail hurt the roof. | The hail damaged the roof. |

## Connect Grammar to Writing

**When you revise your writing, look for verbs that you can change to more exact verbs.**

# Write to Inform

✓ **Voice** When you write an **informational paragraph**, remember to use your own words. Do not copy words that were written by someone else.

Greg drafted a paragraph about thunderstorms. He used facts from *Super Storms*. Later, he revised some sentences to be in his own words.

## Writing Traits Checklist

✓ **Ideas**
Did I use facts instead of opinions?

✓ **Voice**
Did I use my own words?

✓ **Sentence Fluency**
Did I get rid of short, choppy sentences?

✓ **Conventions**
Did I write neatly and leave margins?

## Revised Draft

Thunderstorms bring lots of
^Millions of gallons of rain
rain. ~~They can drop millions of~~
^can fall in one minute.
~~gallons of water in just one~~

~~minute.~~ Lightning bolts destroy

trees and houses.
^Lightning can also start fires in
~~They can also start fires in~~
^trees or grass!
~~forests and grasslands.~~

# Thunderstorms

by Greg Popov

Thunderstorms bring lots of rain. Millions of gallons of rain can fall in one minute. Lightning bolts destroy trees and houses. Lightning can also start fires in trees or grass! People can tell how close lightning is by counting the seconds between lightning and the sound of thunder. For every five seconds you count, the lightning is one mile away.

I made sure I used my own words to tell facts.

## Reading as a Writer

How did Greg tell facts in his own way? What parts of your paragraph can you retell in your own words?

*How Chipmunk Got His Stripes*
Joseph Bruchac & James Bruchac
Pictures by Jose Aruego & Ariane Dewey

*Why Rabbits Have Short Tails*

✔ **TARGET VOCABULARY**

**tunnel**

**curled**

**height**

**direction**

**toward**

**healed**

**brag**

**tease**

Vocabulary Reader      Context Cards

Native American *Folktales*

254

# Vocabulary in Context

- Read each **Context Card**.
- Ask a question that uses one of the Vocabulary words.

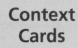

## 1 tunnel

A chipmunk knows how to dig a tunnel, which is a passage underground.

## 2 curled

This fox is curled up around its warm, bushy tail.

### 3 height

An eagle builds its nest at an amazing height. It is at the top of a tall tree.

### 4 direction

An owl can turn its head in any direction. It can look all around.

### 5 toward

These bear cubs run toward their mother so she can protect them.

### 6 healed

This pangolin will go back to the forest when it is well, or healed.

### 7 brag

These antlers are something to brag about! They are huge.

### 8 tease

Never tease, or bother, wild animals. Always respect them.

# Background

**✔ TARGET VOCABULARY** **Folktales** A folktale is a story that people have been telling for many years. Some folktale characters brag about their strength or height. That gets them into trouble. Some characters tease others. That causes trouble, too. A folktale can explain why Bear's injured tail healed as it did or why Squirrel's tail is curled toward its back. It can tell why Mole hid in a tunnel or why certain travelers went in the direction of a village.

**An American Indian tale tells how Coyote brought people fire.**

256

# Comprehension

✔ **TARGET SKILL** **Understanding Characters**

In *How Chipmunk Got His Stripes,* Bear and Brown
Squirrel speak and act like people.  Use story clues and
what you know to figure out why the characters act
that way.  List story clues and your ideas on a chart like
this one.

| Words | Actions | What I Know |
|-------|---------|-------------|
|       |         |             |

✔ **TARGET STRATEGY** **Summarize**

As you read, summarize, or express in your own
words, why Bear and Brown Squirrel act as they do.
Summarizing will help you better understand the story.
If you do not understand, slowly reread the text.

*How Chipmunk Got His Stripes*
Joseph Bruchac & James Bruchac
Pictures by Jose Aruego
& Ariane Dewey

## ✔ TARGET VOCABULARY

| | |
|---|---|
| tunnel | toward |
| curled | healed |
| height | brag |
| direction | tease |

## ✔ TARGET SKILL

**Understanding Characters** Tell more about characters.

| | | |
|---|---|---|
| | | |
| | | |

## ✔ TARGET STRATEGY

**Summarize** Stop to tell important events as you read.

### GENRE

A **folktale** is a story that is often told by people of a country.

## MEET THE AUTHORS

### Joseph Bruchac and James Bruchac

As a boy, Joseph Bruchac listened to his grandfather tell stories of their Native American heritage. Joseph passed these stories down to his son, James. Now this father-and-son team writes books together, such as *Raccoon's Last Race*.

## MEET THE ILLUSTRATORS

### Jose Aruego and Ariane Dewey

These two artists make a great team. When they are working on a book, Jose Aruego first draws the lines for the characters, using pen and ink. Then Ariane Dewey paints the colors. In this way, they have illustrated more than 60 books.

# How Chipmunk Got His Stripes

by Joseph Bruchac and James Bruchac
pictures by Jose Aruego and Ariane Dewey

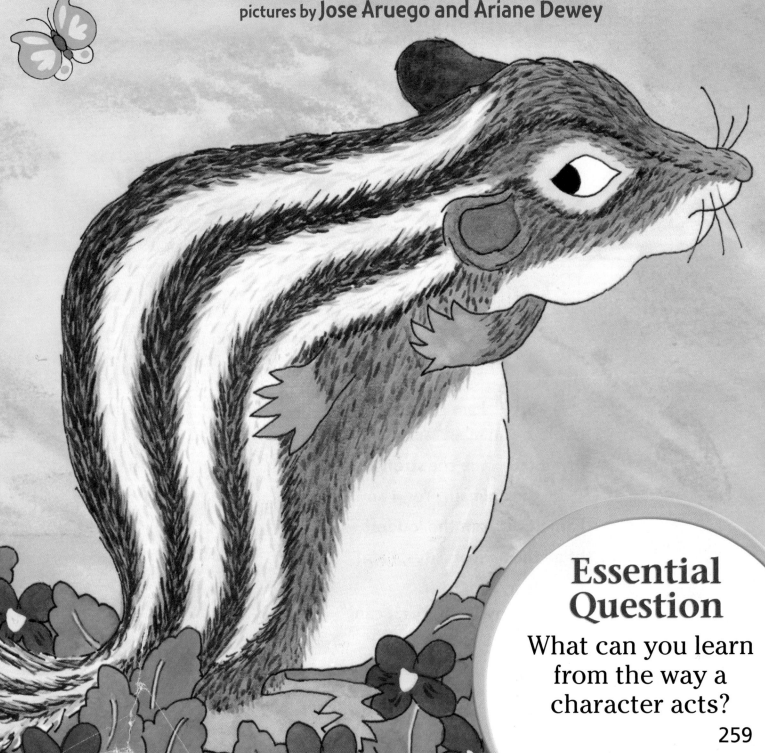

## Essential Question

What can you learn from the way a character acts?

One autumn day long ago, Bear was out walking.
As he walked, he began to brag:

"I am Bear. I am the biggest
of all the animals. Yes, I am!
I am Bear. I am the strongest
of all the animals. Yes, I am!
I am Bear. I am the loudest
of all the animals. Yes, I am!
I am Bear, I am Bear.
I can do anything. Yes, I can!"

As soon as Bear said those words, a little voice spoke up from the ground.

"Can you really do anything?"

Bear looked down. He saw a little brown squirrel, standing on his hind legs.

"Can you really do anything?" Brown Squirrel asked again.

Bear stood up very tall. "I am Bear. I can do anything. Yes, I can!"

"Can you tell the sun not to rise tomorrow morning?" Brown Squirrel asked.

"I have never tried that before. But I am Bear. I can do that. Yes, I can!"

✔ **STOP AND THINK**
**Understanding Characters** What tells you that Bear thinks he is wonderful?

Bear turned west to face the sun. It was the time
when the sun always goes down. Bear stood up to his
full height and spoke in a loud voice.

"SUN, DO NOT COME UP TOMORROW."

At his words, the sun began to disappear behind
the hills.

"You see?" Bear said. "Sun is afraid of me.
He is running away."

"But will the sun come up tomorrow?"
Brown Squirrel asked.

"No," Bear answered. "The sun will not come up!"

Then Bear turned to face east, the direction where the sun always used to come up. He sat down. Little Brown Squirrel sat down beside him. All that night, they did not sleep. All that night, Bear kept saying these words:

"The sun will not come up, hummph!
The sun will not come up, hummph!"

But as the night went on, little Brown Squirrel began to say something, too. He said these words:

"The sun is going to rise, oooh!
The sun is going to rise, oooh!"

All through the night, they sat there. One by one, other animals gathered around them. Fox and Wolf, Deer and Moose, Rabbit and Porcupine, Hawk and Owl, Otter and Beaver, Frog and Turtle, and even the little mice came. They wanted to see who would be right, Bear or Brown Squirrel. This is what the other animals heard:

"The sun will not come up, hummph!"
"The sun is going to rise, oooh!"
"The sun will not come up, hummph!"
"The sun is going to rise, oooh!"

**STOP AND THINK**
**Author's Craft** Why does the author keep repeating Bear's sentence and little Brown Squirrel's sentence?

Finally, it was just before dawn, the time when the sun always used to come up.

"Look," said Turtle, "a little bit of red is starting to show."

"Yes," said Owl. "I believe the sun will rise today."

Bear only chanted louder:

"The sun will not come up, hummph!"

But right next to him, little Brown Squirrel piped up:

"The sun is going to rise, oooh!"

And the sun came up. The birds sang their welcoming songs. The bright light of the new day spread over the land. Everyone was happy except for one animal. That animal was Bear. He sat there with his head down and a grumpy look on his face.

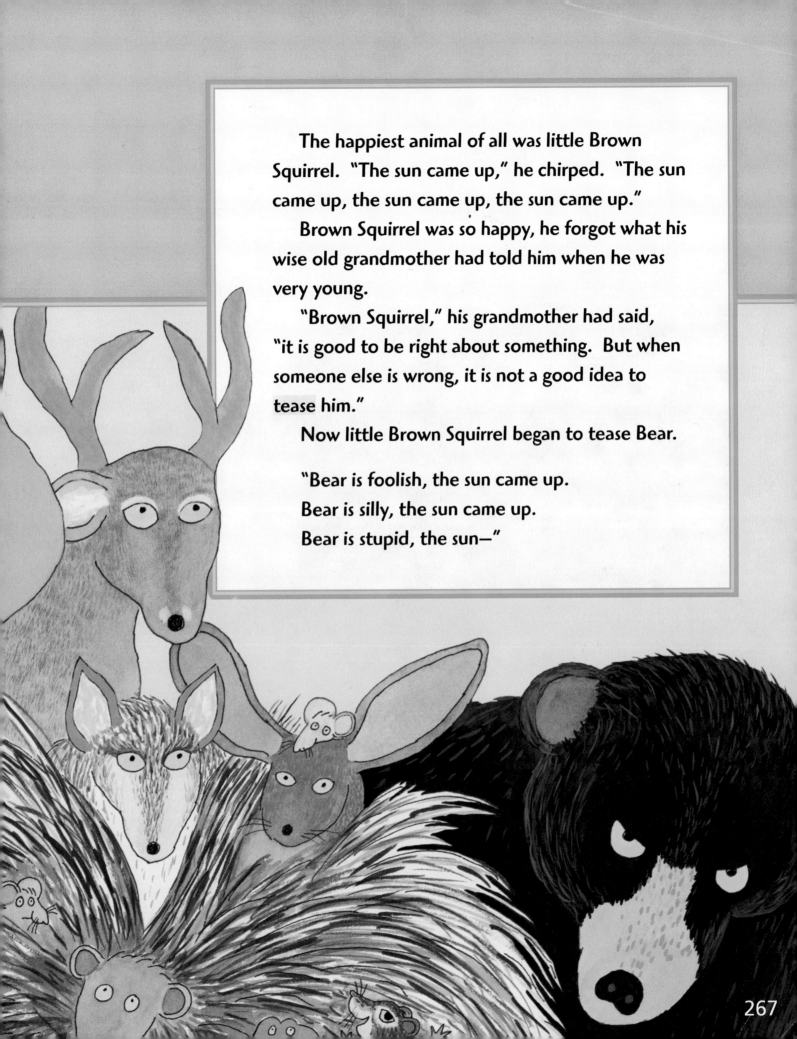

The happiest animal of all was little Brown Squirrel. "The sun came up," he chirped. "The sun came up, the sun came up, the sun came up."

Brown Squirrel was so happy, he forgot what his wise old grandmother had told him when he was very young.

"Brown Squirrel," his grandmother had said, "it is good to be right about something. But when someone else is wrong, it is not a good idea to tease him."

Now little Brown Squirrel began to tease Bear.

"Bear is foolish, the sun came up.
Bear is silly, the sun came up.
Bear is stupid, the sun—"

**WHOMP!**

Bear's big paw came down on little Brown Squirrel, pinning him to the ground. Bear leaned over and opened his huge mouth.

"Yes," Bear growled. "The sun did come up. Yes, I do look foolish. But you will not live to see another sunrise. You will not ever tease anyone else again, because I, Bear, am going to eat you."

Brown Squirrel thought fast. "You are right to eat me," he said. "I was wrong to tease you. I would like to say I am sorry before you eat me. But you are pressing down on me so hard that I cannot say anything. I cannot say anything at all. I cannot even breathe. If you would lift up your paw just a little bit, then I could take a deep breath and apologize before you eat me."

"That is a good idea," Bear said. "I would like to hear you apologize before I eat you."

So Bear lifted up his paw. But instead of apologizing, Brown Squirrel ran. He ran as fast as he could toward the pile of stones where he had his home. He had a tunnel under those stones and a nice warm burrow underground. Little Brown Squirrel's grandmother stood there in the door waiting for him.

"Hurry, Brown Squirrel," she called. "Hurry, hurry!"

**STOP AND THINK**
**Summarize** How did little Brown Squirrel escape from Bear?

Little Brown Squirrel dove for the door to his home. But Bear was faster than he looked. He grabbed for little Brown Squirrel with his big paw. Bear's long, sharp claws scratched Brown Squirrel's back from the top of his head to the tip of his tail.

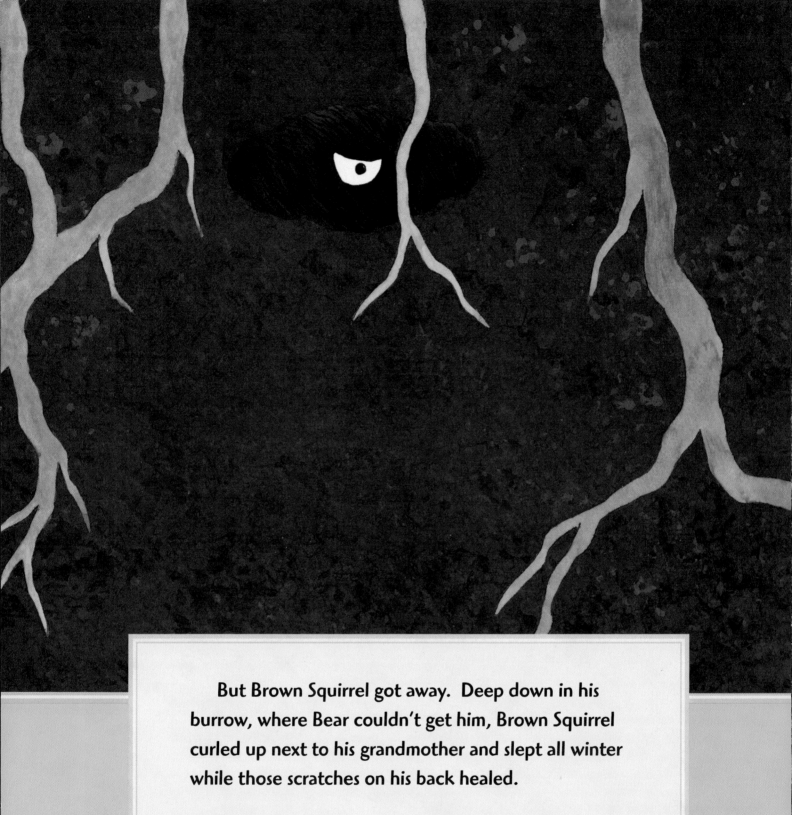

But Brown Squirrel got away. Deep down in his
burrow, where Bear couldn't get him, Brown Squirrel
curled up next to his grandmother and slept all winter
while those scratches on his back healed.

When spring came again, little Brown Squirrel came out of his hole and looked at himself. There were long pale stripes all the way down his back where Bear had scratched him. He was Brown Squirrel no longer. He was now Chipmunk, the striped one.

That is how Chipmunk got his stripes. Ever since then, Chipmunk has been the first animal to get up every morning. As the sun rises, he scoots to the top of the tallest tree to sing his song:

"The sun came up,
the sun came up,
the sun came up,
the sun came up!"

And ever since then, Bear has been the last animal to get up. He doesn't like to hear Chipmunk's song. It reminds him—as it reminds us all—that no one, not even Bear, can do everything.

## Lesson Learned

**Write a Note**

Write a note to Brown Squirrel. Tell what you learned from him about teasing. Make sure you use complete sentences.
PERSONAL RESPONSE

## Turn and Talk — Character Clues

With a partner, look back through the story. Together, make a list of Bear's actions. What do the actions tell you about Bear? Talk about your ideas. UNDERSTANDING CHARACTERS

# Traditional Tales

### ✔ TARGET VOCABULARY

| | |
|---|---|
| tunnel | toward |
| curled | healed |
| height | brag |
| direction | tease |

### GENRE

**Traditional tales** are stories that have been told for many years.

### TEXT FOCUS

A **folktale** is a story that is passed down to explain or entertain.

# Why Rabbits Have Short Tails

**adapted by Gina Sabella**

Once Rabbit had a long, beautiful tail. It curled over his back like a furry fan. Rabbit was taking his family on a trip.

"We have to travel in the direction of the stream," Rabbit said. "When we see the hill with the tallest height, we should head toward it."

When they spotted the tallest hill, Rabbit saw that they would have to swim across the stream.

Rabbit liked to brag. He told everyone how clever he was. He did not tell anyone that he could not swim. He did not want anyone to tease him.

Rabbit saw a turtle crawling out of a tunnel. Ten tiny turtles followed behind.

"You have a large family," Rabbit said.

"Yes," Turtle replied. "My family is the biggest in the woods."

"I'm not sure," Rabbit answered. "My family might be bigger."

"Line up your children across the stream," Rabbit said. "Then I can see who has a bigger family." Soon the turtles were lined up. Rabbit and his family jumped on their backs and skipped across the stream.

Turtle was not happy. He tried to grab Rabbit by the tail. But Rabbit's tail snapped off and he hopped away.

Even after it healed, Rabbit's tail never grew long and beautiful again.

# Making Connections

 **Text to Self**

**Act Out a Lesson** The characters in the stories you just read all learn a lesson. Act out for a partner a lesson you have learned. Have your partner guess what you learned.

 **Text to Text**

**Compare Story Structure** How are the characters, settings, and events in the two selections you just read the same and different? Write a few sentences to explain.

 **Text to World**

**Explore Traditional Tales** Are *How Chipmunk Got His Stripes* and *Why Rabbits Have Short Tails* made-up stories or true stories? Share your ideas with the class.

# Grammar

**Verbs in the Present** A **verb** in the **present** names an action that is happening now. Add *-s* or *-es* to this kind of verb when it tells about a singular noun. Do not add *-s* or *-es* when the verb tells about a plural noun.

**Academic Language**

verb

present

| Verbs After Singular Nouns | Verbs After Plural Nouns |
|---|---|
| The bear sleeps. | Two bears sleep. |
| The animal runs. | Many animals run. |
| The chipmunk rushes. | Some chipmunks rush. |

**Try This!** **Choose the correct verb to complete each sentence. Then write the sentence correctly.**

1. The squirrel (learn, learns) a lesson.

2. Bears (scratch, scratches)!

3. The animal (hide, hides) in a hole.

4. Days (pass, passes) before the animal comes out.

**Sentence Fluency**  To make your writing smoother, join two short sentences with the same subject.  Write **and** between the two predicates to make one longer sentence.

**Short Sentences**

Chipmunks find nuts.

Chipmunks store them for the winter.

**New Sentence with Joined Predicates**

Chipmunks find nuts and store them for the winter.

## Connect Grammar to Writing

**When you revise your instructions next week, try joining two sentences that have the same subject.**

# Write to Inform

☑ **Ideas** Before you write **instructions**, think about the important steps. What does your reader need to know to do this project?

When Alexa planned instructions for making a birdfeeder, she listed important materials and steps. Then she numbered the steps in order in a chart.

## Writing Process Checklist

▶ **Prewrite**

☑ Did I think about my audience and purpose?

☑ Did I choose a topic I know well?

☑ Did I include all the important steps?

☑ Are my steps in the correct order?

**Draft**

**Revise**

**Edit**

**Publish and Share**

## Exploring a Topic

### Things You Need

pinecone

peanut butter

birdseed

spoon

∧paper plate

∧string

### Steps

2 spread peanut butter on pinecone

4 hang on tree

3 roll in birdseed

1 ∧tie string to pinecone

1. Tie a piece of string to a pinecone.

2. Cover the pinecone with peanut butter.

3. Roll the pinecone in birdseed.

4. Hang the birdfeeder in a tree.

When I organized my instructions, I made sure I had all the important steps.

## Reading as a Writer

What helpful steps did Alexa add? Where can you add important steps to your own chart?

✓ TARGET VOCABULARY

**millions**

**choices**

**drift**

**simple**

**weaker**

**wrapped**

**disgusting**

**decide**

Vocabulary
Reader

Context
Cards

# Vocabulary in Context

- Read each **Context Card**.

- Tell a story about two pictures, using the Vocabulary words.

### 1 millions

It looks like this shark has millions of teeth, but it really only has a few dozen.

### 2 choices

Visitors at the aquarium have many choices of things to see.

**3** **drift**

This clever otter will not drift, or float, away.

**4** **simple**

Dolphins make jumping out of the ocean look simple and easy.

**5** **weaker**

One of these crab claws is weaker than the other. It is not very strong.

**6** **wrapped**

The octopus wrapped its strong tentacles around its prey.

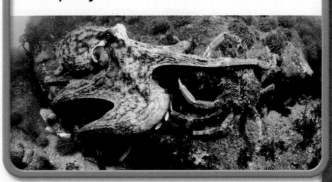

**7** **disgusting**

Yuck! The litter around the trash can smells disgusting!

**8** **decide**

Is this a starfish or a crab? You decide.

# Background

**Ocean Life** Millions of animals live in the oceans. Jellyfish are very simple ocean animals. Stronger animals eat weaker animals. Once an octopus gets its legs wrapped around a clam, the clam will be its lunch. Blue whales eat tiny krill that drift by. Weaker animals have a few choices for protection. Squid squirt clouds of disgusting ink in which they hide. Once a jellyfish stings a turtle, the turtle will decide the jellyfish is not good to eat.

**Oceans of the World**

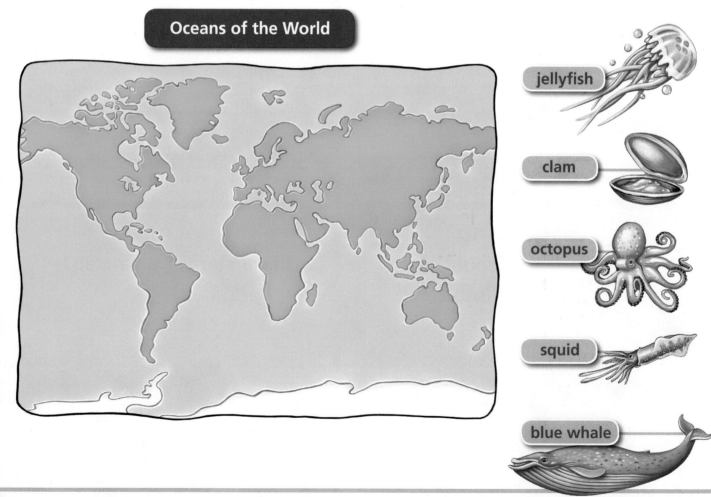

jellyfish

clam

octopus

squid

blue whale

# Comprehension

✔ **TARGET SKILL** **Fact and Opinion**

*Jellies* contains many facts about jellyfish and some opinions. When you read, you must figure out which sentences give facts and which sentences state what the author feels or thinks. A chart like this can help.

| Fact | Opinion |
|------|---------|
|      |         |

✔ **TARGET STRATEGY** **Monitor/Clarify**

As you read, stop to make sure you understand the story details. Readers monitor and clarify, or make sure they understand what they are reading, in order to make sense of new ideas and information. Your chart can help you.

THE LIFE OF JELLYFISH
Twig C. George

### ✔ TARGET VOCABULARY

| | |
|---|---|
| millions | weaker |
| choices | wrapped |
| drift | disgusting |
| simple | decide |

### TARGET SKILL

**Fact and Opinion** Tell if an idea can be proved or is a feeling.

| | |
|---|---|
| | |

### TARGET STRATEGY

**Monitor/Clarify** Find ways to figure out what doesn't make sense.

### GENRE

**Informational text** gives facts about a topic.

**MEET THE AUTHOR**

# Twig C. George

Twig C. George's love of nature began while she was growing up around her mom, writer Jean Craighead George. The George household had many unusual pets, including tarantulas, sea gulls, crows, and a screech owl that liked to take showers. Twig George raises her own children around nature, too.

# Jellies
## THE LIFE OF JELLYFISH

by Twig C. George

If you were a jellyfish you would have two choices—to go up or to go down. That's it. Two. You would not have a brain, so you could not decide what to have for breakfast or where to go for lunch.

Mangrove jellyfish

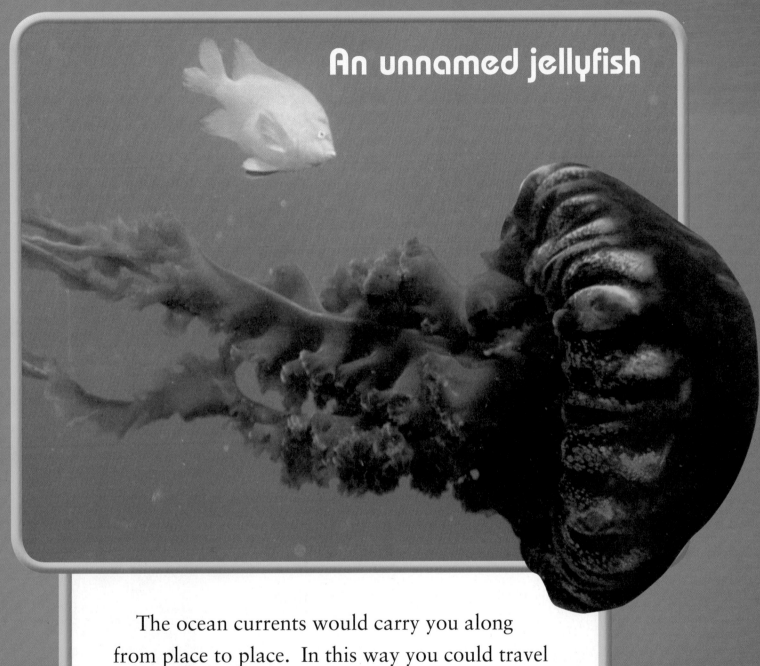

An unnamed jellyfish

The ocean currents would carry you along from place to place. In this way you could travel hundreds of miles. Food might pass by you and get caught in your tentacles. Or not.

## Rhizostone jellyfish

Sea turtles, dolphins, and whale sharks would try to eat you.

You wouldn't worry about it because you couldn't.

You would just float on.

# Comb jellyfish

You would protect yourself with millions of tiny, mechanical cells that, when touched by another animal, release a chemical and sting. Like a bow and arrow. You would not know if you were stinging a friend or an enemy. You would not even know what a friend or an enemy was!

Jellyfish sting for protection and to catch food. That's all. They don't hunt and they can't chase. They just bump and sting. Bump and sting.

Little fish swim in and out of the dome of this moon jellyfish.

Some jellyfish sting gently. Some jellyfish have a sting so powerful that they are more dangerous than a cobra. These are the Australian box jellies.

**Australian box jellyfish**

# Thimble jellyfish

Jellyfish are so simple that they look like plastic trash floating in the sea. When an animal eats a jellyfish it stays healthy and strong. When an animal eats plastic it gets weaker and weaker and eventually dies.

**Upside-down jellyfish**

Some jellyfish lie on the shallow bottom in clear, warm seas and grow their own food. These are called upside-down jellyfish. Once they have eaten small bits of algae, just once, they can grow more inside their bodies by sitting in the sun. They are their own greenhouses and grocery stores all wrapped up in one.

**STOP AND THINK**

**Monitor/Clarify** What do you need to know to understand how upside-down jellyfish get food?

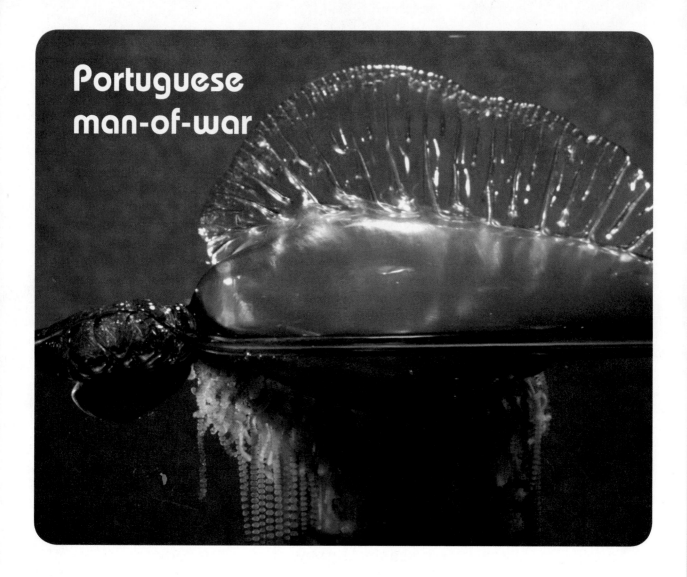

Portuguese man-of-war

To be a jellyfish you need to be shaped like a bell, with at least one mouth, and tentacles. Many animals called jellyfish are really something else. The Portuguese man-of-war is not a real jellyfish. It has an air-filled bubble instead of a water-filled bell.

Jellyfish are almost all water and a little protein. They look slimy and disgusting when they wash up on the beach.

Moon jellyfish

☑ STOP AND THINK
**Fact and Opinion** What is one fact the author gives?

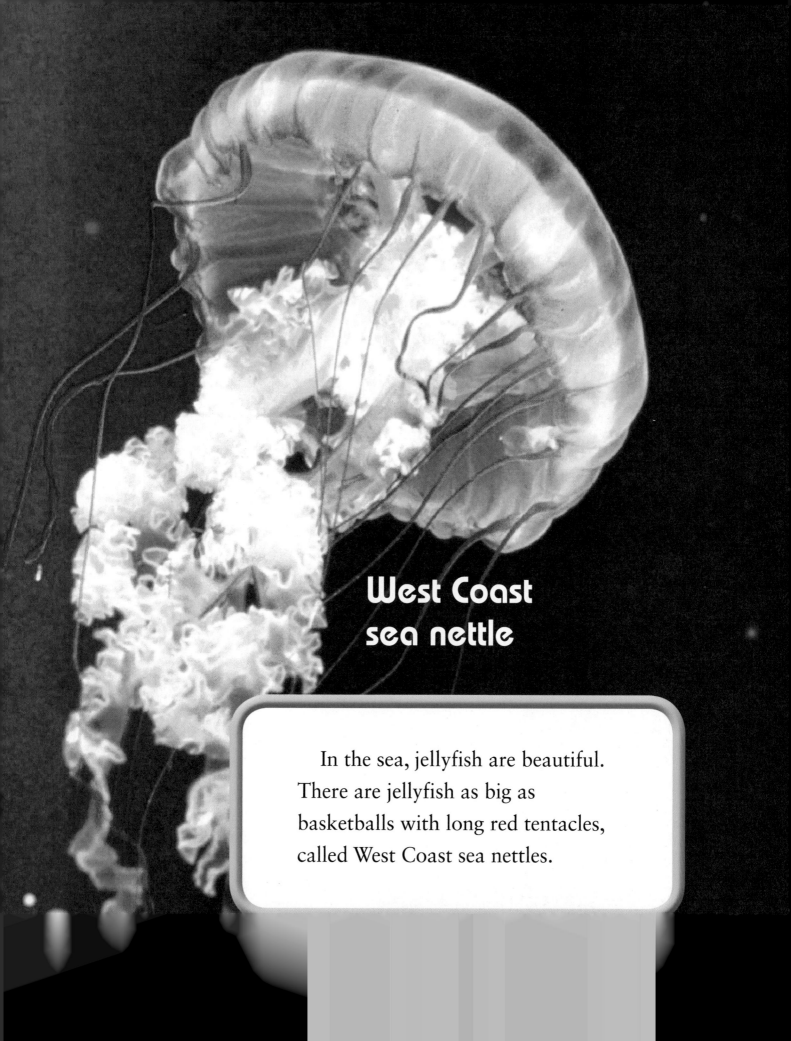

## West Coast sea nettle

In the sea, jellyfish are beautiful. There are jellyfish as big as basketballs with long red tentacles, called West Coast sea nettles.

There are tiny, elegant jellyfish that look like a blizzard of snowflakes.

Oikopleura labradorensis

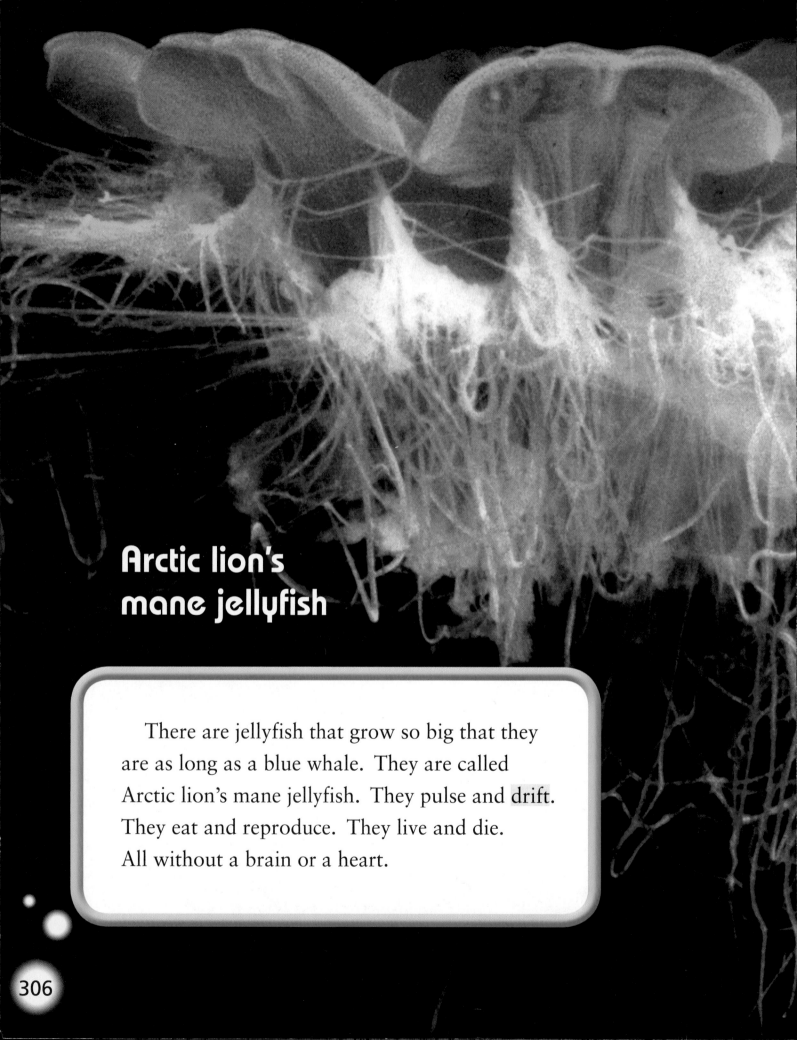

# Arctic lion's mane jellyfish

There are jellyfish that grow so big that they are as long as a blue whale. They are called Arctic lion's mane jellyfish. They pulse and drift. They eat and reproduce. They live and die. All without a brain or a heart.

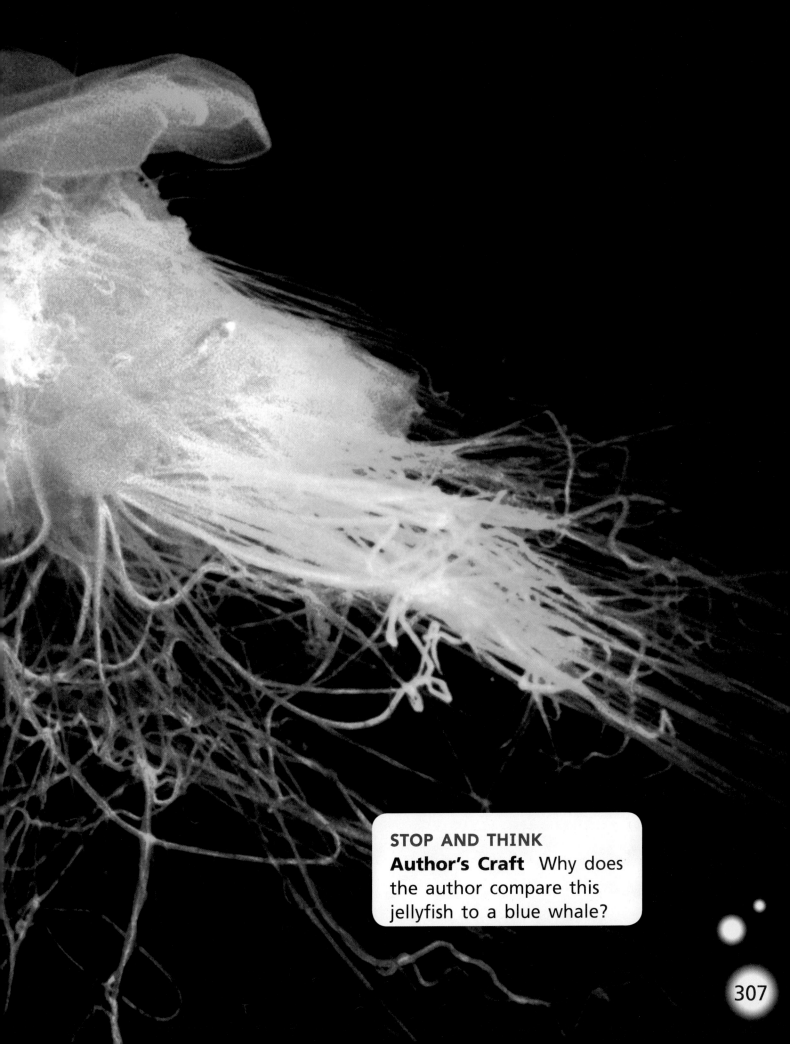

**STOP AND THINK**

**Author's Craft** Why does the author compare this jellyfish to a blue whale?

**Golden Mastigias jellyfish**

Someday you might be very lucky and see an ocean full of jellyfish. And, since you have a brain and a heart, you would know you were seeing something unforgettable.

# Your Turn

## Jiggling Jellies

**Write a Poem**

Think of all you have learned about jellyfish. Then work with a partner to write a poem about them. Make your poem fun. Use as many words as you can that start with the letter *j*. PARTNERS

Jellies wiggle.

Jellies jiggle.

Jellies jet

and get all wet!

## Is That a Fact?

Look through *Jellies*. Find one sentence that is a fact. Find one sentence that is an opinion. Have a partner tell which is which. FACT AND OPINION

## Connect to
# Social Studies

✔ **TARGET VOCABULARY**

| | |
|---|---|
| millions | weaker |
| choices | wrapped |
| drift | disgusting |
| simple | decide |

**GENRE**

**Informational text** gives facts about a topic. This is a social studies text.

**TEXT FOCUS**

A **diagram** is a drawing that shows how something works.

# Meet Norbert Wu

## A Day on the Job

When Norbert Wu goes to work, he grabs his flippers! Why? Mr. Wu works underwater. Millions of creatures live in the water. Wu's job is to take photos of them.

# Choices to Make, Places to Go

Mr. Wu's job is not simple. He has to make a lot of choices. He must decide where to dive. He has to decide what camera to use. Some people might think it would be disgusting to be wet all the time.

Not Mr. Wu. He thinks his job is fun. He lives in California, but sometimes he travels. He has taken photos of Antarctic sea spiders. He has taken photos of Indonesian frogfish. He has seen sea cucumbers drift along the ocean floor and octopuses with their arms wrapped around their prey.

# Dressed for Work

Wu uses special cameras to get the best photos. Check out what he wears to work!

**Air Tank**
This air tank holds the oxygen that Wu breathes.

**Flippers**
Feet are weaker than fins for swimming. Wu wears flippers so he can swim better.

**Camera**
Wu's camera is specially made so he can use it underwater.

# Making Connections

## Text to Self

**Think About Jobs** Would you rather write about ocean animals or take pictures of them? Explain using examples from the selections.

## Text to Text

**Compare Captions** Choose one photo caption from *Jellies* and one from "Meet Norbert Wu." Tell your partner how captions can be alike and different.

## Text to World

**Connect to Science** Choose an ocean animal that you read about in *Jellies* or "Meet Norbert Wu." Use one or two sources of information to research the animal. Share your facts with a partner.

Facts About Sharks

# Grammar

**Verbs in the Present, Past, and Future**
Some **verbs** name actions that are happening now.  Some verbs name actions that happened before, or in the **past**.  Other verbs name actions that will happen later, or in the **future**.

| Present | Past | Future |
|---|---|---|
| The jellies float. | The jellies floated. | The jellies will float. |
| We watch them. | We watched them. | We will watch them. |

**Turn and Talk**  **Work with a partner.  Read the sentences aloud.  Tell whether the action is happening in the present, in the past, or in the future.**

❶ I like ocean animals.

❷ Shelley enjoyed the waves.

❸ The jellies swim all around.

❹ We will visit the zoo tomorrow.

**Sentence Fluency** When you write, make sure your verbs tell about the same time. Your writing will be easier to understand.

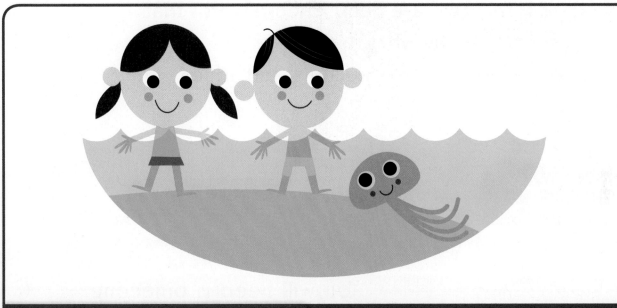

| Incorrect | Correct |
|---|---|
| We play at the beach yesterday. | We played at the beach yesterday. |
| We will jump in the waves yesterday. | We jumped in the waves yesterday. |

## Connect Grammar to Writing

**When you revise your instructions, be sure all your verbs tell about the same time.**

# Write to Inform

☑ **Word Choice** It is easier for readers to follow **instructions** if the steps are clear. Choose words that tell your readers exactly what to do.

Later, Alexa revised her instructions and added exact words.

## Writing Process Checklist

**Prewrite**

**Draft**

▶ **Revise**

☑ Are my steps in order?

☑ Did I use time-order words, such as *first*, *next*, and *finally*?

☑ Did I use exact words to make my steps clearer?

☑ Do I tell my readers what to do with what they made?

**Edit**

**Publish and Share**

## Revised Draft

You will need a pinecone, peanut butter, birdseed, a spoon
~~utensil~~, a paper plate, and string.

First, tie one end of the
                the top
string to ~~part~~ of the pinecone.
~~Cut a long piece of string.~~

# How to Make a Birdfeeder

by Alexa Saperstein

Make an easy and fun birdfeeder. You will need a pinecone, peanut butter, birdseed, a spoon, a paper plate, and string.

First, cut a long piece of string. Tie one end of the string to the top of the pinecone. Next, take a spoon, scoop some peanut butter, and spread it all over the pinecone. Then pour some birdseed on a paper plate. Roll the pinecone around in the birdseed.

I added exact words to make my instructions clearer.

## Reading as a Writer

Which exact words did Alexa add to make her steps clear? Where can you add exact words to your own instructions?

317

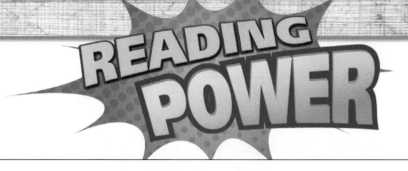

Read the next two selections. Think about how the characters act and feel.

# Snow Day

It was Friday morning. Katie was still asleep. Suddenly she felt her sister jump onto her bed. Katie groaned as she looked at the clock. It was too early.

"Get up!" said Maddie. "You have to see this."

Katie got up and went to the window. She saw a strange sight. There was a lot of snow! The girls had seen a few flakes before, but this was unusual.

"Let's make a snowman!" Katie shouted.

# Tornado!

Last summer, we had a scary surprise. It was a hot, humid night. It looked as if there would be a thunderstorm. Suddenly, the sky turned yellow. Then we heard a strange sound. It sounded like a train.

"A tornado is coming!" my dad said. My whole family ran down to the basement. We were happy when it was over. As we climbed the stairs, we began to feel anxious. We were about to find out what had happened.

A lot of trees were down. There were branches everywhere. Our neighbors had lost a part of their roof. Luckily, no one was hurt.

# Unit 2 Wrap-Up

## The Big Idea

**Nature in a Box**  Start a nature museum.  Get a shoebox or another container.  Collect things at a park that are part of nature.  Display your nature collection in the box.  Label each item.

## Listening and Speaking

**Listen and Look**  Sit quietly outside and close your eyes. Make a list of sounds you hear that come from things in nature.  Then open your eyes.  List the things you see that are part of nature. Which things are the same?

# Tell Me About It

## Unit 3

# Big Idea

We learn from
each other.

# Paired Selections

**TARGET VOCABULARY**

**understand**

**gathered**

**impatient**

**impossible**

**believe**

**problem**

**demand**

**furious**

Vocabulary
Reader

Context
Cards

# Vocabulary in Context

- Read each **Context Card**.

- Use a Vocabulary word to tell about something you did.

### 1 understand

These children talk to each other with their hands. They understand sign language.

### 2 gathered

The students gathered around the computer in order to see the screen.

### 3 impatient

This girl looks impatient. She is tired of waiting so long.

### 4 impossible

It is impossible to hear when there is so much noise.

### 5 believe

People clap if they believe, or feel, someone has done a good job.

### 6 problem

Raise your hand if you have a problem or need help.

### 7 demand

These lights and sirens demand that everyone get out of the way.

### 8 furious

Babies cry when they are angry. This baby is furious!

# Background

**Reaching an Agreement**

Students believe they should get a longer recess.
It seems like an impossible wish. They should not get
impatient or furious, though. They should not demand
a longer recess, either. Once students have gathered
with teachers, calm thinking and talking can lead to
ideas. Then everyone can understand why a longer
recess is a good plan. Problem solved!

How to Reach an Agreement

Present the request.

Meet to discuss ideas.

Agree on a solution.

# Comprehension

✔ **TARGET SKILL**  **Conclusions**

In *Click, Clack, Moo*, the author wants you to draw conclusions.  She wants you to use story clues to fill in more details than she gives.  Use a chart like this to write a conclusion about Farmer Brown or his animals.  List the story clues that helped.

✔ **TARGET STRATEGY**  **Infer/Predict**

Use your conclusions about Farmer Brown and the other animals to infer, or figure out, more about their thoughts and feelings.  Your conclusions may also help you to predict what might happen next!

✔ **TARGET VOCABULARY**

| | |
|---|---|
| understand | believe |
| gathered | problem |
| impatient | demand |
| impossible | furious |

✔ **TARGET SKILL**

**Conclusions** Use details to figure out more about the text.

✔ **TARGET STRATEGY**

**Infer/Predict** Use clues to figure out more about story parts.

**GENRE**

**Humorous fiction** is a story that is written to make the reader laugh.

**MEET THE AUTHOR**

# Doreen Cronin

When Doreen Cronin was a kid, her dad used to tell funny stories. One night several years ago, she woke up and wrote *Click, Clack, Moo.* "It made me laugh, just like my father used to do," she says.

**MEET THE ILLUSTRATOR**

# Betsy Lewin

If you were to visit Betsy Lewin at home, you'd find paint tubes, brushes, paper, and a kitty named Sophie on her drawing table. In her travels, Ms. Lewin has seen gorillas in Uganda, elephants in Botswana, and tigers in India.

# CLICK, CLACK, MOO
## Cows That Type

by Doreen Cronin          pictures by Betsy Lewin

Farmer Brown has a problem.

His cows like to type.

All day long he hears

Click, clack, **moo.**
　　Click, clack, **moo.**
Clickety, clack, **moo.**

At first, he couldn't believe his ears.
Cows that type?
Impossible!

Click, clack, **moo.**
   Click, clack, **moo.**
Clickety, clack, **moo.**

Dear Farmer Brown,
The barn is very cold at night.
We'd like some electric blankets.
Sincerely,
The Cows

It was bad enough the cows had found the old typewriter in the barn, now they wanted electric blankets! "No way," said Farmer Brown. "No electric blankets."

So the cows went on strike. They left a note on the barn door.

Sorry.
We're closed.
No milk today.

**STOP AND THINK**
**Conclusions** How does Farmer Brown feel about the notes? How do you know?

"No milk today!" cried Farmer Brown.
In the background, he heard the cows
busy at work:

Click, clack, **moo.**
  Click, clack, **moo.**
Clickety, clack, **moo.**

**The next day, he got another note:**

Dear Farmer Brown,
The hens are cold too.
They'd like electric blankets.
Sincerely,
The Cows

The cows were growing **impatient** with the farmer. They left a new note on the barn door.

"No eggs!" cried Farmer Brown. In the background he heard them.

Click, clack, **moo.**
   Click, clack, **moo.**
Clickety, clack, **moo.**

"Cows that type. Hens on strike! Whoever heard of such a thing? How can I run a farm with no milk and no eggs!" Farmer Brown was furious.

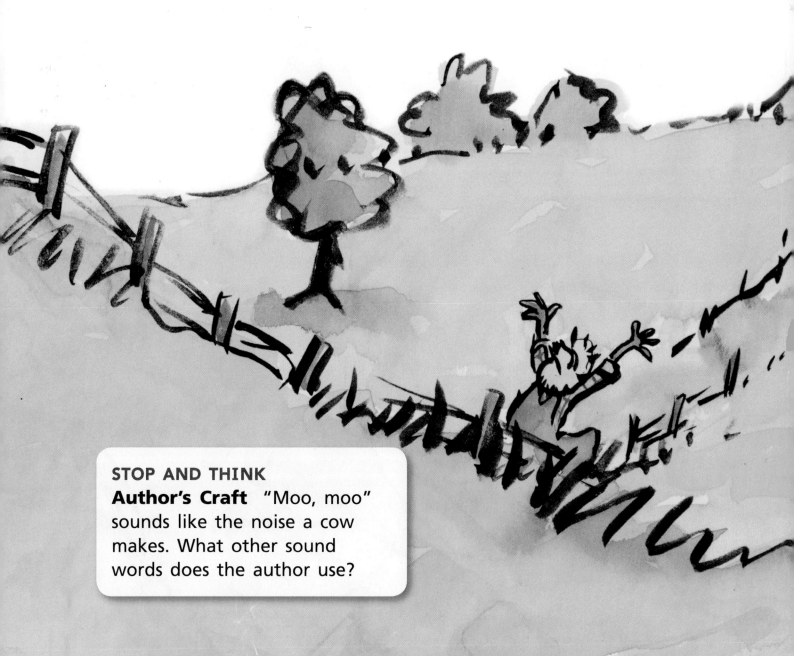

STOP AND THINK
**Author's Craft** "Moo, moo" sounds like the noise a cow makes. What other sound words does the author use?

**Farmer Brown got out his own typewriter.**

Dear Cows and Hens:
There will be no electric blankets.
You are cows and hens.
I demand milk and eggs.
Sincerely,
Farmer Brown

Duck was a neutral
party, so he brought the
ultimatum to the cows.

The cows held an emergency meeting. All the animals gathered around the barn to snoop, but none of them could understand Moo.

All night long, Farmer Brown waited for an answer.

Duck knocked on the door early the next morning. He handed Farmer Brown a note:

Dear Farmer Brown,
We will exchange our typewriter
for electric blankets.
Leave them outside the barn door
and we will send Duck over with
the typewriter.
Sincerely,
The Cows

Farmer Brown decided this was a good deal. He left the blankets next to the barn door and waited for Duck to come with the typewriter.

342

**The next morning, he got a note:**

Dear Farmer Brown,
The pond is quite boring.
We'd like a diving board.
Sincerely,
The Ducks

Click, clack, **quack.**
   Click, clack, **quack.**
Clickety, clack, **quack.**

**STOP AND THINK**
**Infer/Predict**  Will the ducks get a diving board?
Check your prediction on the next page.

## Animals Ask

### Act It Out

Work with a partner. Choose a farm animal other than a cow or a duck. What might the animal want from Farmer Brown? Act out what might happen when the animal asks Farmer Brown for something. Take turns being Farmer Brown and the animal.

PARTNERS

 ## Duck's Plan

Read the last page of the story again. Why didn't Duck return the typewriter? Share your ideas with a partner. Tell what clues helped you figure it out.

CONCLUSIONS

# Talk About Smart Animals!

**by Donald Logan**

You may think only animals in storybooks or movies do things that seem impossible. You would be wrong!

Meet Rio and Alex. They are real-life animals. Rio is a sea lion. Alex is a parrot. These animals can do things that most people would never believe animals like them could do.

## This Sea Lion Can Match

Rio is not like any other sea lion. She can solve a simple problem and tell the answer to her trainers!

Rio has learned to look at three pictures and decide which two are most alike. First, Rio's trainers show her one picture. Rio studies it. Then her trainers add two more pictures. Rio points her nose at the picture that goes best with the first one she saw. When Rio is right, she gets a tasty treat.

Rio is not impatient. She takes her time before she answers.

Rio is deciding which two of these pictures are most alike.

347

## Not Bad for a Bird Brain!

Alex is an African grey parrot. Grey parrots in the wild are often seen gathered together in large groups. In the wild, parrots communicate using bird calls and other sounds. Alex is special because he has learned to talk. He knows over one hundred words!

Alex's owner has also taught Alex to tell colors apart and to count. Alex can even understand questions and answer them.

Sometimes Alex gets tired. He becomes furious and will demand a treat. After a break, he goes right back to solving problems.

"Want a nut!"

# Making Connections

## Text to Self

**Connect to Science** What can the animals in the selections do that most animals cannot do? What would you like to teach an animal to do? Explain the steps to a partner. Have your partner repeat the steps.

## Text to Text

**Compare Stories** Doreen Cronin wrote *Click, Clack, Moo: Cows That Type* and *Diary of a Spider* (Lesson 4). Explain how the settings and the events of these stories are the same and different.

## Text to World

**Write a Letter** Think about the letters that the cows wrote. Write your own letter asking an adult family member for something. Be sure to include all the parts of a letter.

# Grammar

**Kinds of Sentences** A **statement** tells something and ends with a period. A **question** asks something and ends with a question mark. A **command** tells a person or animal to do something and ends with a period.

| Statement | Question | Command |
| --- | --- | --- |
| I wrote a note. | Did you write a note? | Please write a note. |

**Turn and Talk** **Work with a partner. Read each sentence aloud. Tell whether it is a statement, question, or command.**

1. Have you been to a farm?

2. She loves cows.

3. Please share the milk.

4. The hens lay eggs.

**Sentence Fluency** A run-on sentence is really two sentences that should not be joined together. If you see a run-on sentence in your writing, turn it into two shorter sentences.

| Run-on Sentences | Separate Sentences |
|---|---|
| Cows are important they give us milk | Cows are important. They give us milk. |
| Do you drink lots of milk | Do you drink lots of milk? |
| I drink three glasses a day. | I drink three glasses a day. |

## Connect Grammar to Writing

**When you revise your persuasive letter, fix run-on sentences by turning each one into two sentences.**

# Write to Persuade

When you write a letter to persuade, be sure your goal is clear to your reader.

Kurt drafted a **persuasive letter**. Later, he revised it to say clearly his reason for writing. Use the Writing Traits Checklist to revise your writing.

## Writing Traits Checklist

**✓ Ideas**
Did I state my goal clearly?

**✓ Organization**
Did I use the parts of a letter? Did I tell things in an order that makes sense?

**✓ Voice**
Does my writing tell how I feel?

**✓ Conventions**
Did I capitalize and punctuate the heading, greeting, and closing correctly?

### Revised Draft

Dear Auntie Lorrie,

I'm writing to ask you ~~for~~ to send me some of your old children's books. ~~something.~~ It's for a really good cause.

Kurt Atchley
244 Austin St.
Ojai, CA  03023

January 24, 2010

Dear Auntie Lorrie,

I'm writing to ask you to send me some of your old children's books.  It's for a really good cause.  We are trying to replace some of the books in our classroom that have fallen apart.  Can you help us?  I hope so.

Love,
Kurt

> I made sure my goal was stated clearly.

## Reading as a Writer

**What did Kurt change to make his goal clearer?  What can you add or change to make your goal clearer?**

✓ **TARGET VOCABULARY**

**shake**

**smooth**

**hours**

**alone**

**real**

**museum**

**nursery**

**whenever**

Vocabulary
Reader

Context
Cards

# Vocabulary in Context

● **Read each Context Card.**

● **Make up a new sentence that uses a Vocabulary word.**

**1**

### shake

Maracas make sounds when you shake them back and forth.

**2**

### smooth

This violin makes a gentle, smooth sound. It doesn't hurt your ears!

### 3 hours

Learning to play an instrument well takes many hours of practice.

### 4 alone

Playing alone, or by yourself, is very special.

### 5 real

A real guitar is louder than a pretend guitar.

### 6 museum

This very old instrument is in a museum. Many people come to see it.

### 7 nursery

A nursery, or baby's room, is a good place to play soft music.

### 8 whenever

The band plays whenever the conductor signals them to.

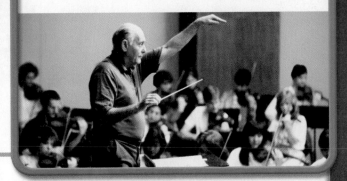

# Background

**What Is a Band?** Sometimes people play music alone. Whenever people play music in a group, they form a band. Some bands play soft, smooth music. This music is good for quiet places, such as a museum or a baby's nursery. Other bands play loud, lively music. This music makes people want to shake their hands and feet and dance to the beat. Being part of a real band takes many hours of practice, but it is also lots of fun!

# Comprehension

**Story Structure**

In *Violet's Music*, the main character has a problem, and she tries to solve it. Use a story map such as this one to keep track of the story structure as you read. Tell who is in the story, where it takes place, and what happens.

✔ **TARGET STRATEGY** **Question**

What problem does the main character face? How does she solve it? As you read, think of more questions about *Violet's Music*. Then read on to find answers. Asking and answering questions helps you make sense of the story.

| | |
|---|---|
| shake | real |
| smooth | museum |
| hours | nursery |
| alone | whenever |

✔ **TARGET SKILL**

**Story Structure** Tell the setting, character, and plot in a story.

✔ **TARGET STRATEGY**

**Question** Ask questions about what you are reading.

**GENRE**

**Realistic fiction** is a story that could happen in real life.

**MEET THE AUTHOR**

# Angela Johnson

As a college student, Angela Johnson used to baby-sit for Cynthia Rylant's son. One day Angela showed the famous author a story she had written. Cynthia liked it so much that she helped get it published, and soon Angela became an author, too.

**MEET THE ILLUSTRATOR**

# Laura Huliska-Beith

Laura Huliska-Beith has held many jobs. She has been a paper carrier, a library aide, and a waitress. She almost became a bus driver. By far her favorite job is illustrating books.

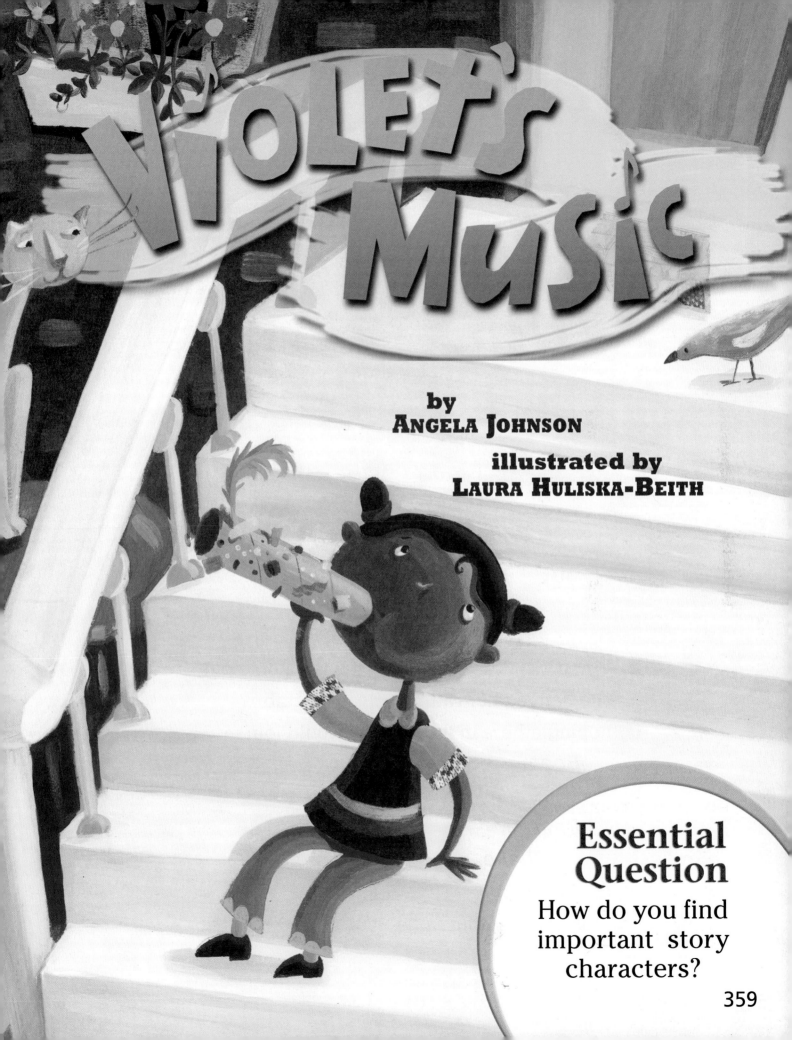

# Violet's Music

by
**ANGELA JOHNSON**

illustrated by
**LAURA HULISKA-BEITH**

## Essential Question

How do you find important story characters?

When Violet was a baby, just a few hours old,
she banged her rattle against the crib,
hoping others in the nursery would join in.
  *Boom*
    *Shake*
  *Beat*
    *Shake*
All day long,
Violet played that rattle.

Could she find other babies to play along?
No, she couldn't.
But she'd keep looking.
Violet played her music all alone.

On Violet's second birthday
Aunt Bertha brought gifts
and a box full of paper, crayons,
glitter, and glue
to make horns that would wail . . .

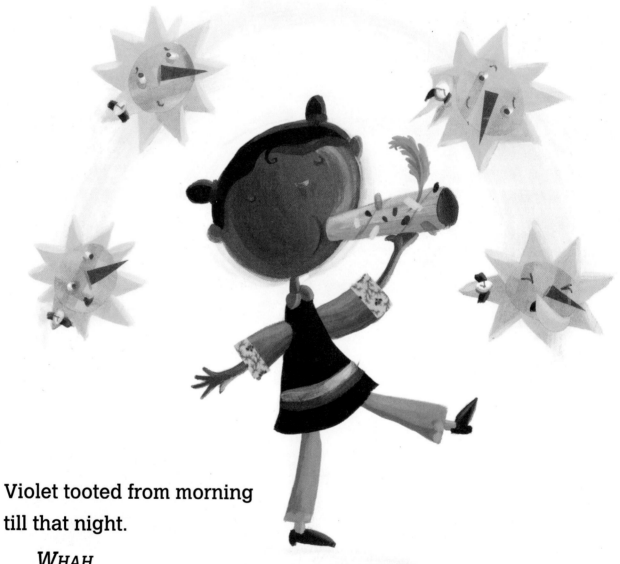

Violet tooted from morning
till that night.

   *W*HAH

      *Woo*

         *Woo*

All day long.

> **STOP AND THINK**
> **Author's Craft** Why do you think the author includes so many words that begin with *b* in the first sentence?

She tried to get everyone to toot
with her all day.

  *WHAH*

    *Woo*

      *Woo*

Oh yeah.
Violet blew that horn.

Could she get her family
to play with her?
No, she couldn't.
But she'd keep on looking.
Violet blew her horn all alone.

Violet wondered in kindergarten
if there were other kids like her,
who dreamed music,
thought music,
all day long.

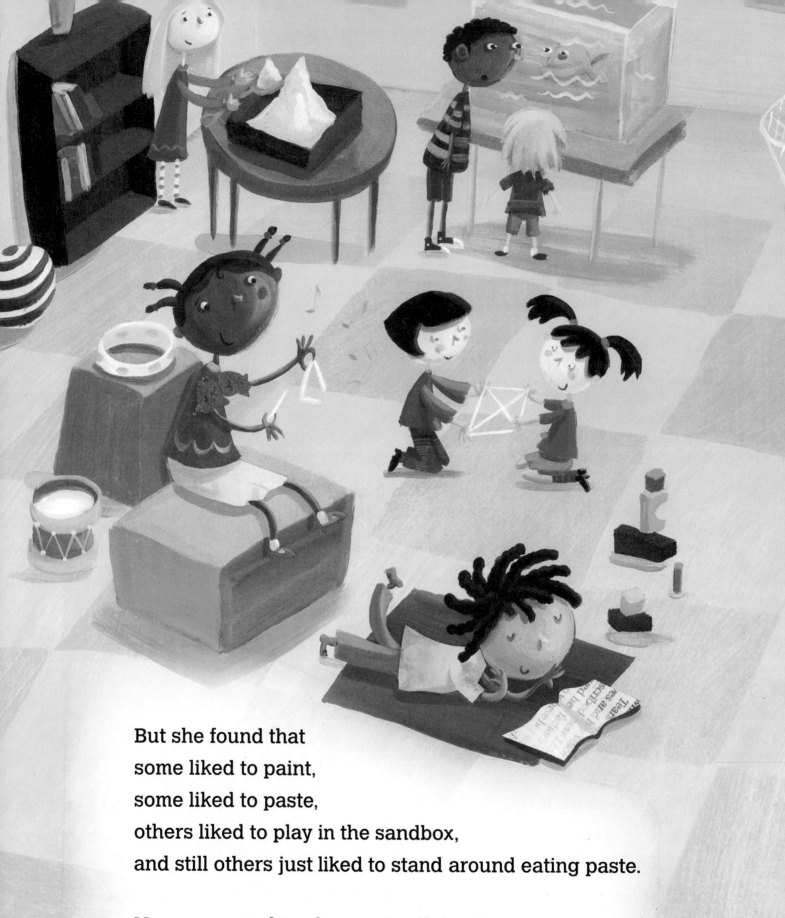

But she found that
some liked to paint,
some liked to paste,
others liked to play in the sandbox,
and still others just liked to stand around eating paste.

No one wanted to play music all day long.

One day at the beach
Violet played with a badminton racket,
a pretend guitar,
hoping someone would join in.

*Plink*
    *Plink*
*Pluck*
    *Pluck*
Violet played guitar.

Could she find a fellow guitarist
buried in the sand?
No, she couldn't.
But she'd keep looking.
Violet played her guitar all alone.

**STOP AND THINK**
**Question** Why is it important
that Violet look for kids like her?

With Violet, you see, it was music all the time.

Breakfast time . . .

Dinner time . . .

Bath time . . .

And all times in between.

Whenever she walked down the street
or hid behind the market's vegetable bins,
or sat on the fire escape,
Violet was always looking for kids like her.

Could she find them at the zoo?
Nope.

At the museum?
Too quiet.

And forget about the dentist.

But she'd keep looking.
Violet and her music, always looking.

Until . . .
one day a few summers later,
Violet was playing her guitar
(a real one now)
in the park.

*Twang*
*Twang*
*Yeah*
*Yeah*
*Twang Twang*
*Yeah!*

When, over by the fountain,
someone started beating a drum …

Then, behind the jungle gym,
a saxophone blew real smooth …

And over beside the flower garden,
someone started to sing …

✔️ **STOP AND THINK**
**Story Structure** Where does Violet finally find kids like her?

370

Now Angel, Randy, and Juan
are in Violet's band.
And if you ask any of them
whether they thought they'd find each other,
they'll say,
"Oh, yeah, we did, we knew we would.

'Cause when we were
in the nursery,
then were two,

and later in kindergarten
and at the beach,
we kept on looking
for kids playing music too!"

Shake TWANG Plink Pluck Whah Woo YEAH!

# Your Turn

## Finding Friends

### Make a Poster

Violet shared her music with her friends. Think of an activity you would like to share with your friends. Make a poster to persuade your friends to join you. Write one or two sentences that describe the activity. PERSONAL RESPONSE

Join me for an art party!

## Turn and Talk — Who's Important?

Work with a partner. List all the characters from the story. Then circle the two or three you think are most important. Tell what clues you used to figure it out. STORY STRUCTURE

# Wolfgang Mozart

## Child Superstar
### by Mark Bechelli

Most little children don't play real music.
Babies might shake a rattle in the nursery.
A five-year-old might bang a drum.

**1750**

**1756** Wolfgang is born in this house in Austria. The house is now a museum.

Wolfgang Amadeus Mozart lived over two hundred years ago. From the time he was very young, Wolfgang was different from most children.

When Wolfgang was three, he would sit alone and play the harpsichord for hours. A harpsichord is an instrument like a piano. By the time Wolfgang was five, he could play slow and smooth or loud and fast. He even wrote his own songs all by himself!

# Wolfgang Mozart's Early Life

**1760**

**1770**

**1759** Wolfgang learns to play the harpsichord.

**1763–1766** Wolfgang plays music all over Europe with his family.

Soon, everyone in Austria was talking about the talented child. Wolfgang played in castles and big concert halls. Whenever he performed, people were amazed. Wolfgang was becoming a musical superstar!

**Wolfgang Mozart at age 6**

# Making Connections

 **Text to Self**

**Activities with Friends** What does Violet like to do with her friends? Do you enjoy any of those activities with your friends? Write a few sentences to explain.

 **Text to Text**

**Have a Conversation** Imagine you and a partner are Violet and Mozart. Have a conversation about how you are alike and different.

 **Text to World**

**Connect to Social Studies** Do you think that Violet likes to play music for special events? What songs do you know that people sing at special times? Discuss your ideas with a partner.

# Grammar

**Kinds of Sentences** All sentences begin with capital letters. Statements and commands end with periods. Questions end with question marks. An **exclamation** shows strong feeling and ends with an **exclamation point**.

| Statement | Question | Command | Exclamation |
|---|---|---|---|
| She plays drums. | Does she play drums? | Stop playing the drums. | I love to play drums! |

**Try This!** **Write each sentence correctly.**

➊ we are so excited to hear the band

➋ what is the name of their band

➌ that flute is old

➍ please play a little louder

378

**Sentence Fluency** In your writing, you may use too many short, choppy sentences. You can fix this by joining sentences that go together to make one longer sentence. Write the word **and** between the sentences. Put a comma before **and**.

### Short, Choppy Sentences

Lupe plays the tuba.

Her brother Jaime plays the flute.

### Longer, Smoother Sentence

Lupe plays the tuba, and her brother Jaime plays the flute.

## Connect Grammar to Writing

**When you revise your opinion paragraph, look for short sentences that you can join with a comma and the word and.**

# Write to Persuade

When you write to persuade, you share your opinions with readers.

Han wrote an **opinion paragraph** about why he likes soccer. Later, he revised his draft to show how much he cares about the sport.

## Writing Traits Checklist

✔ **Ideas**
Did I use details and examples to explain my reasons?

✔ **Organization**
Did I state my opinion at the beginning of my paragraph?

✔ **Voice**
Does my writing show how I feel about my subject?

✔ **Sentence Fluency**
Did I vary the length of my sentences?

### Revised Draft

love

I ~~like~~ soccer. This game has something for everyone! It is easy to learn, so anyone can play. It is great exercise. People all over the world play soccer. I watch games with my brother.

each weekend

# Soccer for Everyone

by Han Choi

I love soccer. This game has something for everyone! It is easy to learn, so anyone can play. It is great exercise. People all over the world play soccer. I watch games with my brother each weekend. We have so much fun when our favorite team wins. I think all children should play soccer.

I added sentences to show how I feel about my subject.

## Reading as a Writer

What did Han add to let you know how he feels about his subject? What can you add to your writing to let your reader know how you feel?

Around the World
**Schools**

**School Poems**

✓ **TARGET VOCABULARY**

**culture**

**community**

**languages**

**transportation**

**subjects**

**lessons**

**special**

**wear**

Vocabulary Reader

Context Cards

One Room Schools

# Vocabulary in Context

- Read each **Context Card**.

- Talk about a picture. Use a different Vocabulary word from the one in the card.

**1**

### culture

Culture is the traditions and beliefs of a group of people.

**2**

### community

A community is a group of people who live together in a certain area.

## 3 languages

People use different languages to write and to speak to one another.

## 4 transportation

People use transportation to get from one place to another.

## 5 subjects

Science is one of the subjects taught in school.

## 6 lessons

This teacher gives lessons to his students. The students learn from each lesson.

## 7 special

These students go to a special school for music. They play music every day.

## 8 wear

These two students wear uniforms at school.

# Background

**✓ TARGET VOCABULARY** **School Days** Not all schools are the same. Some have their students wear uniforms. Some have special transportation, such as school buses. Others allow students to get their lessons over the Internet. Most schools teach different subjects. Students taking social studies may learn about their own community or a different culture. Many schools teach different languages as subjects. All schools are places where students learn!

Many American schools have classrooms like this one.

# Comprehension

## ✔ TARGET SKILL  Author's Purpose

An author may write to make you smile, to tell you facts, or to explain ideas. What is the author's purpose for writing *Schools Around the World*? Keep track of details on a chart like this one to figure out the author's purpose.

## ✔ TARGET STRATEGY  Analyze/Evaluate

Think carefully about the selection details and the author's purpose for writing *Schools Around the World.* Use your own ideas to decide whether the author has done a good job of telling about different schools.

Around the World
**Schools**

✓ **TARGET SKILL**

**Author's Purpose**
Tell why an author writes a book.

✓ **TARGET STRATEGY**

**Analyze/Evaluate**
Tell how you feel about the text, and why.

**GENRE**

**Informational Text** gives facts about a topic. Set a purpose for reading based on the genre.

**MEET THE AUTHOR**

# Margaret C. Hall

Margaret C. Hall has written many nonfiction books for children. Her books include topics from national parks to mallard ducks. *Schools Around the World* is part of a series of books she wrote. Other books in the series include *Homes Around the World* and *Games Around the World*.

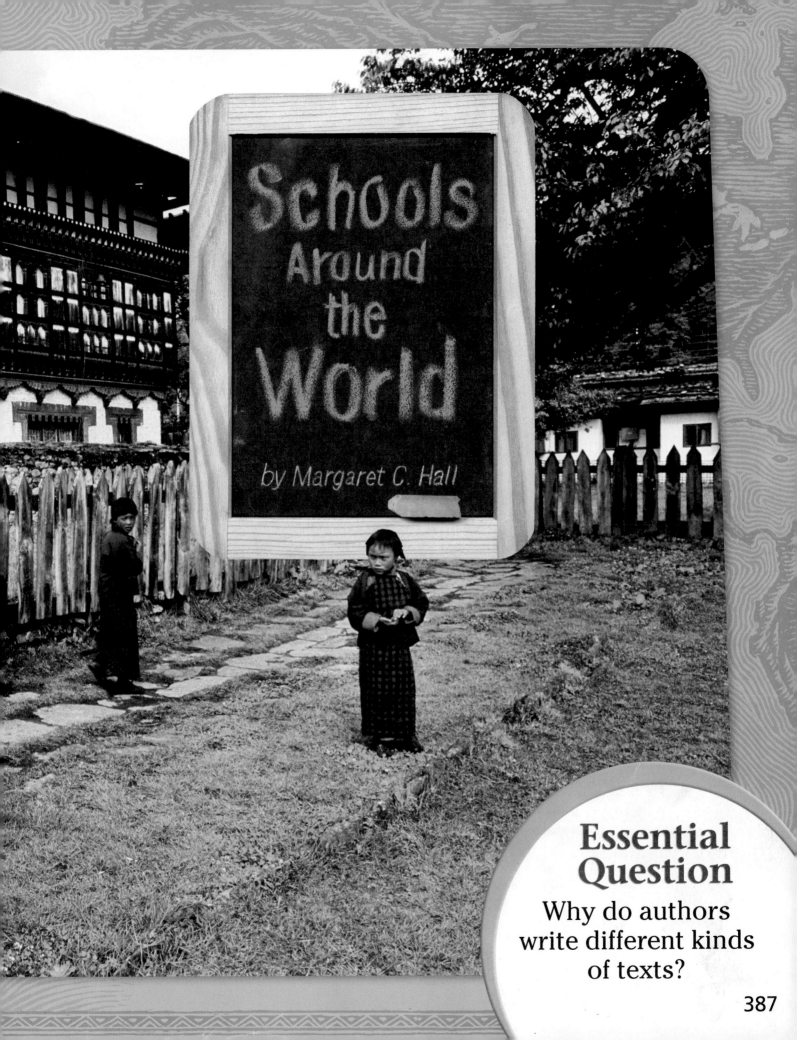

Schools
Around
the
World

by Margaret C. Hall

# Schools Around the World

All around the world, children go to school.
Some children spend most of their day at school.
Others spend only a few hours there.

*Some school buildings in Asia are tall, like this one.*

*These students in an American classroom start their day by saying the Pledge of Allegiance.*

Schools are different in different parts of the world. But they are all the same in one way. Schools are where children go to learn.

### AMAZING SCHOOL FACTS

*A long time ago, a German man started a new kind of school. He thought that small children should grow like flowers in a garden. He called his school kindergarten. The word means "children's garden" in German.*

*These students in Tibet, China, are about to start their morning classes.*

# School Buildings

The kind of school buildings children have depends on where they live. It depends on the climate and the resources of their community.

School buildings can be large or small. They can be made from many different materials. Some children even go to school outside or in buildings with no walls.

**AMERICAN SCHOOL FACTS**

*Schools have been around for thousands of years. The first schools were started to teach children about their culture.*

# Getting to School

Children travel to school in many different ways. The kind of transportation they use depends on where they live. It also depends on how far they have to go.

Many children walk or ride bicycles to school. Others ride in cars, on buses, or on a train. Some children go to school by boat.

**AMAZING SCHOOL FACTS**

*In some places, children live too far away from their school to go there. Teachers give lessons over the radio or by using computers that are hooked up to the school.*

✔ **STOP AND THINK**
**Author's Purpose** Do you think the author is trying to tell facts or tell a story about transportation? Explain.

# School Clothing

Children around the world wear different kinds of clothing to school. What they wear often depends on the climate where they live. It also depends on what season it is.

In some schools, the students all dress alike. They wear uniforms. Students from different schools have different uniforms.

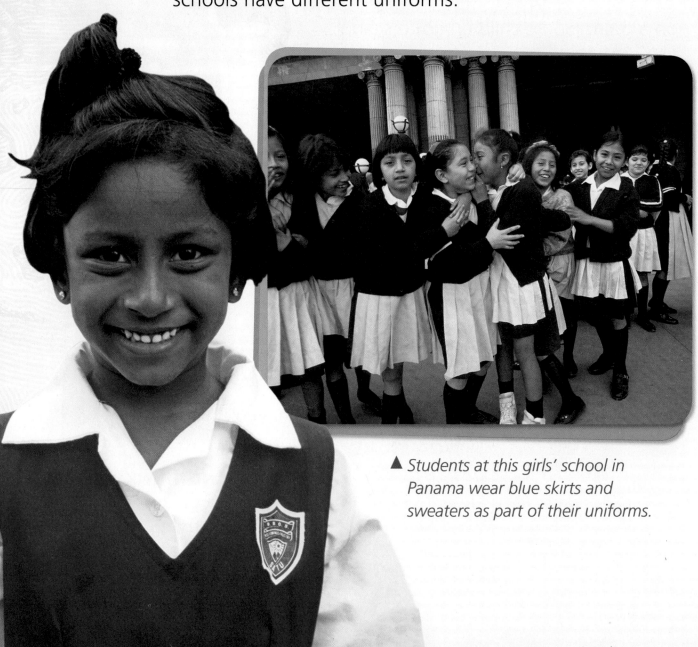

▲ Students at this girls' school in Panama wear blue skirts and sweaters as part of their uniforms.

392

*These students in Germany are learning science on a class trip with their teachers.*

# The School Day

All around the world, teachers help students learn new things. Children do some schoolwork in groups. They do other schoolwork on their own.

Most children eat lunch or a snack at school. They may also have time to play. At many schools, children take class trips, too.

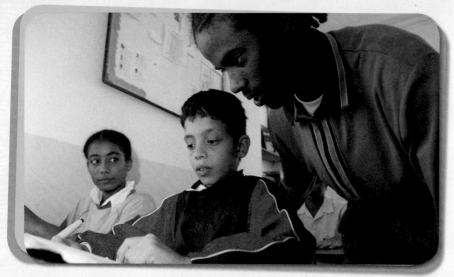

*This teacher answers a question for his student at a school in Cuba.*

# Learning to Read and Write

One important job for teachers is to help children learn to read and write.  Students learn to read and write in many different languages.

The language children use at school depends on where they live.  Some children study their own language and another language, too.

**STOP AND THINK**
**Author's Craft** How do the captions help the author tell about different schools?

At an American school overseas, students study a map of Europe.

# Other Lessons

Children learn many things at school. All around the world, they study math and science. They learn about their own country and other countries, too.

Many children around the world study art and music in school. They may also learn how to use a computer.

*These students in Great Britain practice playing music at school.*

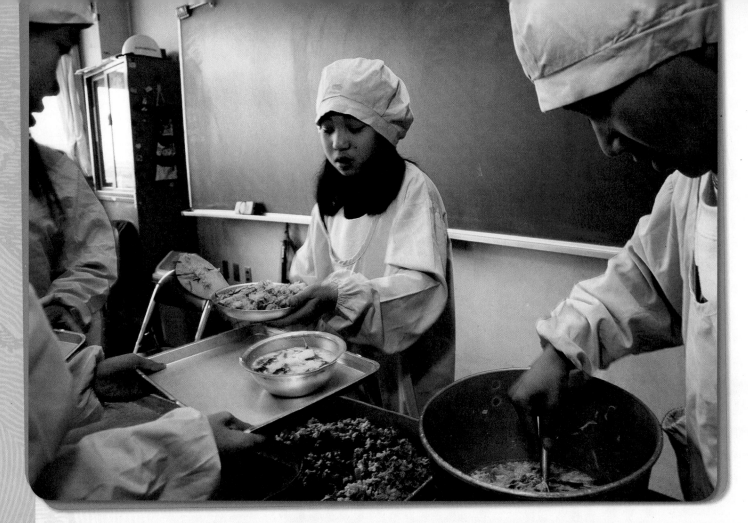

*In this school in Japan, students help serve lunch.*

# School Chores

Most children have chores to do at school. They help to keep the classroom neat and clean. They may even help to set up the classroom every day.

In some places, children work to keep the schoolyard neat and clean. Some children may serve lunch to one another.

*This teacher gives extra help to students after school.*

# After School

Some children go to school even after the school day is over. They may have a tutor to help them with the subjects that are harder for them.

Some children have other lessons after school. They study things they cannot learn in school. They may learn about dance, music, or their own culture.

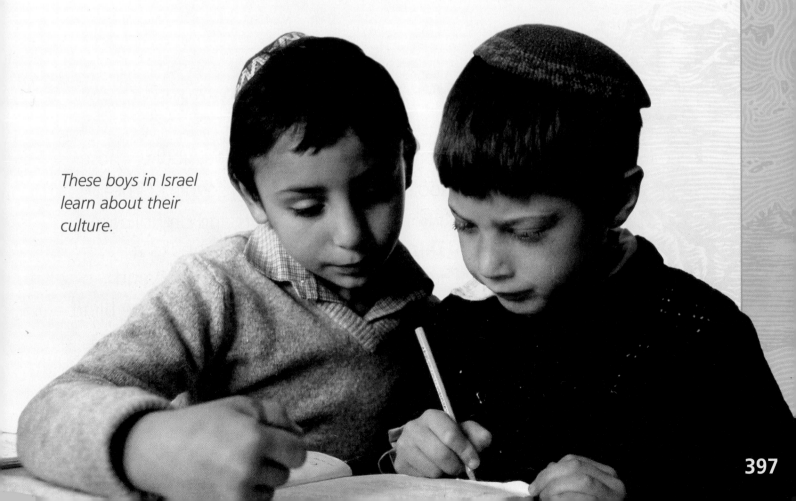

*These boys in Israel learn about their culture.*

*Students at this boarding school eat, study, and live together.*

# Special Schools

Some children live at their schools. These schools are called boarding schools. The children go home for visits and on holidays.

This girl cannot see. She goes to a school where she can learn to read and write in a special way. People who are blind read with their fingers. They use a system of raised dots called Braille.

# Home Schooling

A home can also be a school.  Some parents teach their children at home.  They want to decide exactly what their children will learn.

People at schools will often help parents plan home lessons for their children.  Many children who study at home go to a school for gym or art classes.

*This mother is teaching her daughter at home.*

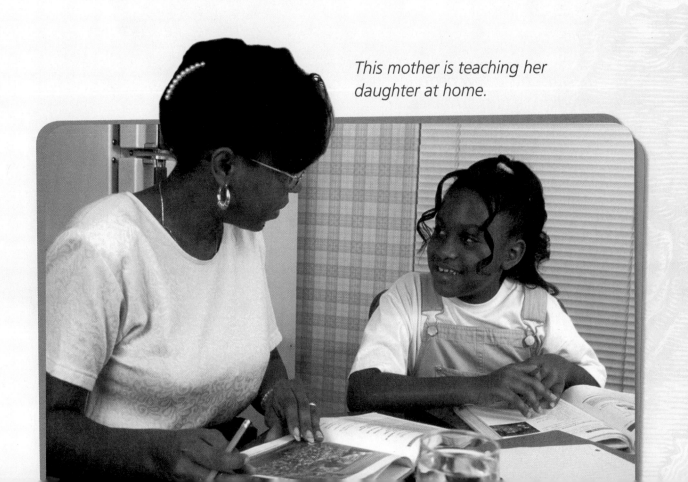

# School and Work

Some children work as performers. They spend part of their day practicing the work that they do. They spend the rest of the day studying regular school subjects.

The students below perform a traditional Russian dance.

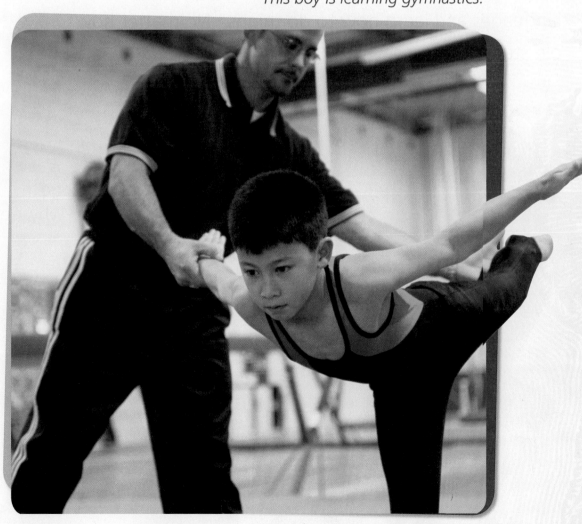

**AMAZING SCHOOL FACTS**

*One of the subjects that was taught in ancient Greece was gymnastics. The ancient Greeks thought gymnastics was just as important to learn as math or reading!*

*This boy is learning gymnastics.*

# Older Students

*These women in India go to school at night.*

Many people go to school even after they are adults. They may go to college. Or, they may go to a trade school to learn how to do a certain job.

Adults also take classes for fun. They study different languages and learn how to do things. No matter how old students are, they go to school to learn.

**STOP AND THINK**
**Analyze/Evaluate** Is it good for adults to go to school? Why or why not?

# Your Turn

## Cool School Facts

**Write About Schools**

Look back through *Schools Around the World*. Find facts that are interesting to you. Then write sentences that tell two ways schools are alike and two ways schools are different. Draw pictures to go with your sentences.

COMPARE AND CONTRAST

All schools help people learn.

**Turn and Talk** ── ## How Authors Work

Work with a partner. Talk about why the author of *Schools Around the World* used facts and photos. Why did the author not use opinions and drawings?

AUTHOR'S PURPOSE

School
Poems

# School Poems

You learn about many subjects in school. You may have lessons in math, about your community, or even about another culture.

The poems here are about school. Listen for rhythm and rhyming words as you read.

## School

Wakes up early.
Just can't wait
to see who's coming.
*Don't be late!*

*by Dee Lillegard*

# The Best

The best part
of the day
is when I hear
the teacher say,
"Sit by my chair
while I read."

We sprawl
on the rug.
It's like listening
to a hug,
while the story magic
pours over me.

*by Kay Winters*

# I Have to Write a Poem for Class

I have to write a poem for class
But don't think I'll succeed.
I know I don't know all the words
That I am going to need.
I cannot quite imagine
How my poem's supposed to be —
I've got a sinking feeling
I'm not good at poetry.

My poem must have a meter,
And it also has to rhyme.
It's due tomorrow morning . . .
How I wish I had more time!
I do not think that I can write
A poem the way I should —
But look . . . this is a poem right here,
And it is pretty good.

*by Jack Prelutsky*

## Write a School Poem

Use rhyming words and rhythm to write your own poem about school. Try to include the words **wear**, **transportation**, **languages**, and **special** in your poem.

# Making Connections

 **Text to Self**

**Draw and Label** Fold a piece of paper in half. Draw a school from *Schools Around the World* on one half. Draw your own school on the other half. Write a label on each picture that describes the school.

 **Text to Text**

**Write a Poem** Choose one of the headings from *Schools Around the World* as a topic for a poem. Then choose two rhyming words from the poems in "School Poems." Use the rhyming words to write a poem about the topic you chose.

 **Text to World**

**Connect to Social Studies** With a small group, choose one of the countries you read about in *Schools Around the World*. Use books and other sources to find out more about schools in that country. Make a poster that shows what you learn.

# Grammar

**Quotation Marks** When you write, show what someone says by putting **quotation marks** (" ") at the beginning and end of the speaker's exact words.

---

### Rules for Using Quotation Marks

Put a **comma** after words such as *said* and *asked.*

> The teacher said, "Take out your math books."

Begin the first word inside the quotation marks with a **capital letter**.

> Mike said, "We are having a quiz today."

Put the **end mark** inside the quotation marks.

> Liza asked, "Who is the class leader?"

---

**Try This!** **Write each sentence correctly. Include quotation marks to show the exact words someone said or asked.**

1. The bus driver said stay in your seats.

2. Jack asked how long is the trip?

3. The teacher said it will take an hour.

**Conventions** You have read stories in which people talk to each other. This makes a story more interesting. Make your own writing more interesting by showing the words people speak.

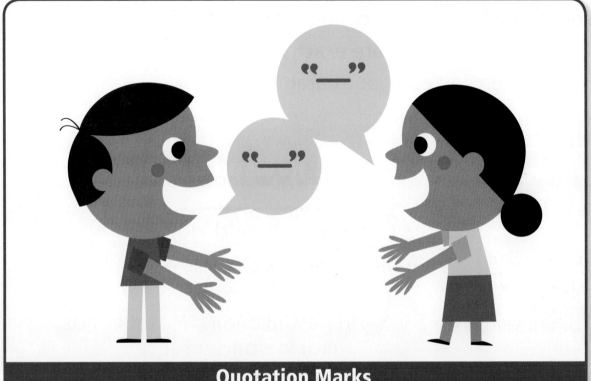

**Quotation Marks**

Nita asked, "What is your favorite subject in school?"
Raj said, "My favorite subject is science."

## ✏ Connect Grammar to Writing

**When you edit your persuasive paragraph, be sure to use commas, capital letters, and end marks correctly.**

# Write to Persuade

When you write to persuade, use exact words to make your writing more interesting.

Rachel wrote a **persuasive paragraph** asking her teacher to take her class to a museum. Later, she revised her writing to use more exact words. Use exact words when you edit your paragraph.

## Writing Traits Checklist

✓ **Organization**
Did I state my opinion at the beginning?

✓ **Word Choice**
Did I use exact words to make my writing interesting?

✓ **Voice**
Did I choose reasons that are important to my audience?

✓ **Sentence Fluency**
Did I begin my sentences in different ways?

## Revised Draft

Our class should go to the Children's Museum.

The Children's Museum has many wonderful ~~lots of nice~~ displays. One display shows how food gets from the farm to the market. We're learning about that in Social Studies right now.

# Let's Take a Trip!

by Rachel Wollmer

Our class should go to the Children's Museum. The Children's Museum has many wonderful displays. One display shows how food gets from the farm to the market. We're learning about that in Social Studies right now. We could write a research paper about what we learn at the museum. Everyone would have a fun day together, too!

> I used exact words to make my writing interesting to my readers.

## Reading as a Writer

Which exact words did Rachel add? What words can you add to make your writing more interesting?

## ✓ TARGET VOCABULARY

**knowledge**

**curious**

**motion**

**silence**

**illness**

**imitated**

**darkness**

**behavior**

| Vocabulary Reader | Context Cards |
|---|---|
|  | |

# Vocabulary in Context

● **Read each Context Card.**

● **Ask a partner a question that uses one of the Vocabulary words.**

**1 knowledge**

Knowledge, or information, can come from books and many other places.

**2 curious**

You can search the Internet if you are curious, or want to learn, about sea animals.

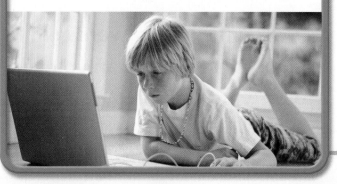

### 3 motion

A hand held up is a motion to stop!

### 4 silence

The rule in the library is "Silence! Please don't speak."

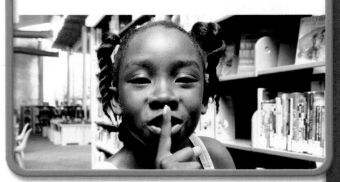

### 5 illness

This child has an illness, but she won't be sick for long.

### 6 imitated

This girl imitated, or copied, her teacher to learn sign language.

### 7 darkness

Flashlights help people see better in darkness.

### 8 behavior

Taking a telephone message is good behavior. It is a polite way to act.

# Background

✓ TARGET VOCABULARY **Braille and Keller** Louis Braille was a curious child. Risky behavior led to an accident and an illness that took away his sight. In school Louis had to read books to gain knowledge. He created a writing system he could read through the motion of his fingertips across a page. Years later, Helen Keller's life imitated Louis's in some ways. Helen lived in both darkness and silence. Reading books with the system Braille invented helped her learn about the world.

Louis Braille developed the Braille system in 1824, when he was fifteen years old.

# Comprehension

✔ **TARGET SKILL** **Main Ideas and Details**

When you read *Helen Keller*, you will learn details
about her childhood. Use those details to figure out
main, or important, ideas that the author gives. Show
a main idea about Helen's life on a chart like this. List
the details that make the main idea clearer.

✔ **TARGET STRATEGY** **Summarize**

As you read, use the main ideas to summarize the
important parts of Helen's life. Then use your summary
to figure out the topic. Tell how the topic is different
from the main idea.

Helen Keller

✔ **TARGET VOCABULARY**

| | |
|---|---|
| knowledge | illness |
| curious | imitated |
| motion | darkness |
| silence | behavior |

✔ **TARGET SKILL**

**Main Ideas and Details** Tell important ideas and details about a topic.

✔ **TARGET STRATEGY**

**Summarize** Stop to tell important ideas as you read.

**GENRE**

A **biography** tells about events in a person's life.

**MEET THE AUTHOR**

*Jane Sutcliffe*

The library was Jane Sutcliffe's favorite place to visit when she was a kid. She says she loved reading biographies "just to get a peek at how other people lived day to day, in different times and places." Now she writes biographies.

**MEET THE ILLUSTRATOR**

*Robert Papp*

Most of Robert Papp's clothes are covered in oil paint. That's because he's extremely messy when he paints. Mr. Papp lives in Pennsylvania with his wife, Lisa, who is also an artist. She's not quite as messy as he is, though.

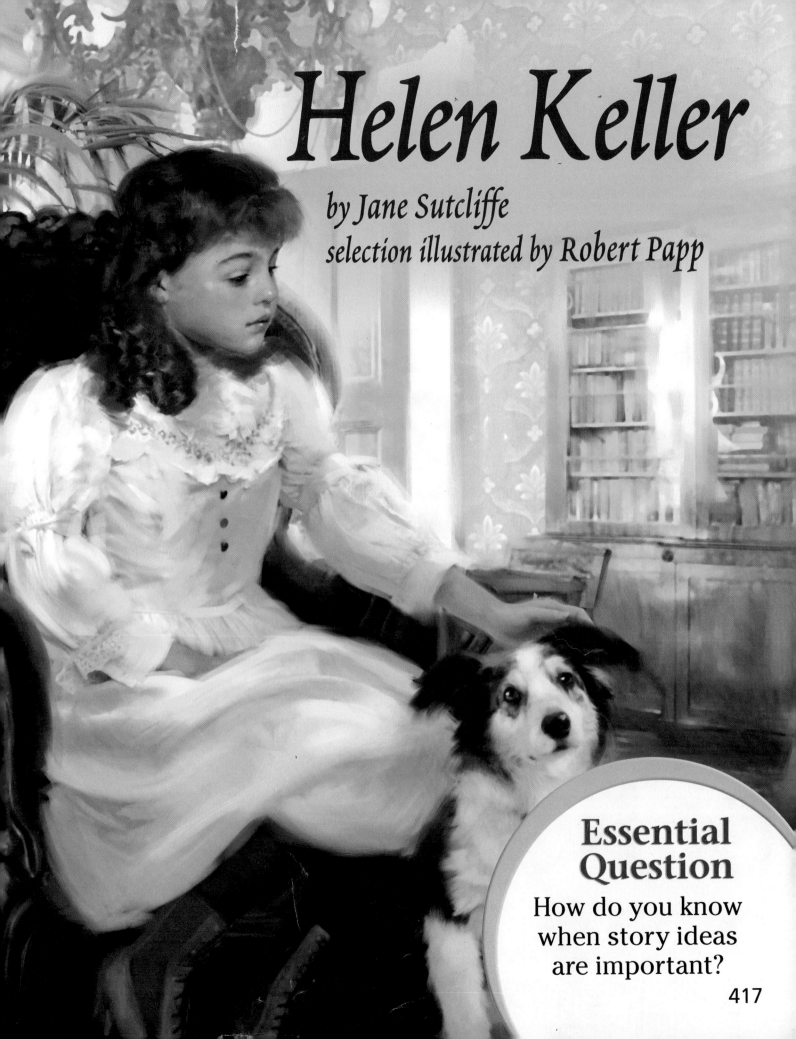

# Helen Keller

by Jane Sutcliffe

selection illustrated by Robert Papp

**Essential Question**

How do you know when story ideas are important?

# Tuscumbia, Alabama
## 1886

Helen Keller reached out. She touched warm, coarse hair. Her busy fingers moved farther down. They felt something smooth and wet. Slap! A hairy tail smacked into Helen's face.

Helen could not see her family's milking cow. But she liked touching it. Helen Keller had been blind and deaf for most of her life. The only way she knew the world was by touch, taste, and smell.

Helen was born in 1880 in Tuscumbia, Alabama. When she was just a baby, she became very sick. The illness took away her sight and hearing. Helen could not hear her brothers' laughter or her mother's voice. She could not see her father's smile or the pretty flowers outside her window. For Helen, there was only silence and gray darkness.

To learn to speak, children need to hear words. But Helen could not hear anything. So she could not speak. Instead, she made motions. When she wanted her mother, she put her hand against her face. When she wanted her father, she made the motion of putting on a pair of glasses. When she was hungry, she pretended to slice and butter bread.

Helen Keller

Helen knew she was different from the rest
of her family. They moved their lips when they
wanted things. Sometimes Helen stood between
two people as they talked. She held her hands to
their lips. Then she tried moving her own lips.
But still no one understood her.

STOP AND THINK

**Main Ideas and Details** How did
Helen know that she was different
from the rest of her family?

That made Helen angry. Sometimes she screamed and cried and kicked for hours. She threw things and hit people. But it didn't change anything. She was still alone in silence and darkness.

Helen was hard to control. Her parents didn't know how to help her. They took her to doctors. None of the doctors could help Helen see or hear again. When Helen was six, a doctor suggested the Kellers visit Alexander Graham Bell. Dr. Bell was famous for inventing the telephone. He also taught deaf people.

Alexander Graham Bell

Dr. Bell told the Kellers to write to Michael Anagnos in Boston. Mr. Anagnos was the head of the Perkins Institution for the Blind. He believed Helen could learn how to let out the thoughts locked inside her. Mr. Anagnos promised to send Helen a teacher.

Michael Anagnos

# Helen and Teacher
## March 1887

Helen's teacher came to live with the Kellers that spring. Her name was Annie Sullivan. Annie had studied at the Perkins School. She was nearly blind herself. Annie needed to control Helen's wild behavior so she could teach her. But Helen did not understand that Annie wanted to help her. For two weeks, Helen fought with Annie. She hit Annie and knocked out one of her front teeth. She even locked Annie in an upstairs room. Mr. Keller had to get a ladder and let Annie out through a window.

Annie Sullivan

Still, Annie did not give up. Little by little, Helen learned to trust her new teacher. Annie began to teach Helen about words. She spelled words using her fingers. Her hand formed a different shape for each letter. She pressed each shape into Helen's hand. When she gave Helen some cake, she spelled C-A-K-E into Helen's palm. When Helen held her doll, Annie spelled D-O-L-L for Helen. Helen imitated the shapes. She thought it was a game. She didn't know that the shapes spelled words.

After a month, Helen could spell whatever Annie spelled. But Helen still did not know that she was naming the things she touched.

**STOP AND THINK**
**Summarize** How did Annie teach Helen about words?

Annie finger spelling into Helen's hand

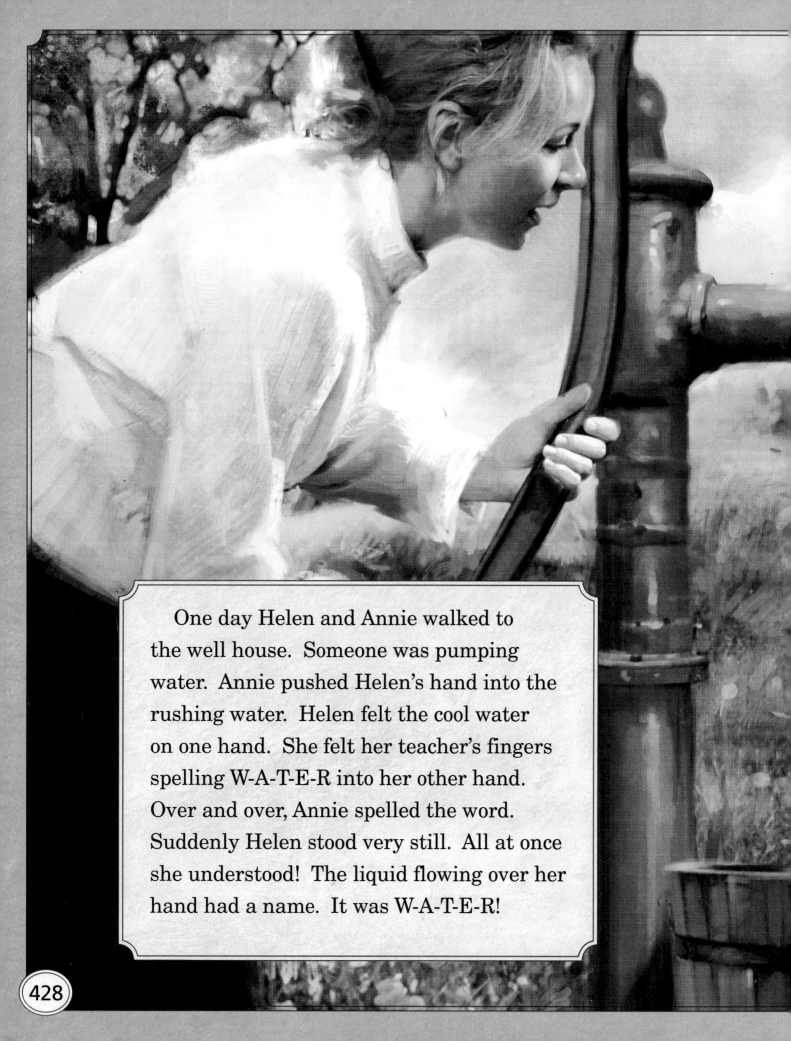

One day Helen and Annie walked to
the well house. Someone was pumping
water. Annie pushed Helen's hand into the
rushing water. Helen felt the cool water
on one hand. She felt her teacher's fingers
spelling W-A-T-E-R into her other hand.
Over and over, Annie spelled the word.
Suddenly Helen stood very still. All at once
she understood! The liquid flowing over her
hand had a name. It was W-A-T-E-R!

Everything had a name! Helen wanted to learn them all. She ran from one thing to another. Annie spelled the name of everything Helen touched. Then Helen turned and pointed to Annie. T-E-A-C-H-E-R, spelled Annie. From then on, Helen's name for Annie was "Teacher." That summer, Helen learned a lot of new words. She stopped using her old motions. Her fingers gave her all the words she needed.

Annie did not teach Helen words one at a time. She talked to her in full sentences. That way, Helen learned more than just new words. She learned new ideas. Helen and Annie took long walks through the woods and along the river. Annie gave Helen lessons on the walks. She showed Helen how seeds sprout and plants grow. She made mountains out of mud and taught Helen about volcanoes. Sometimes they climbed a tree and had a lesson there.

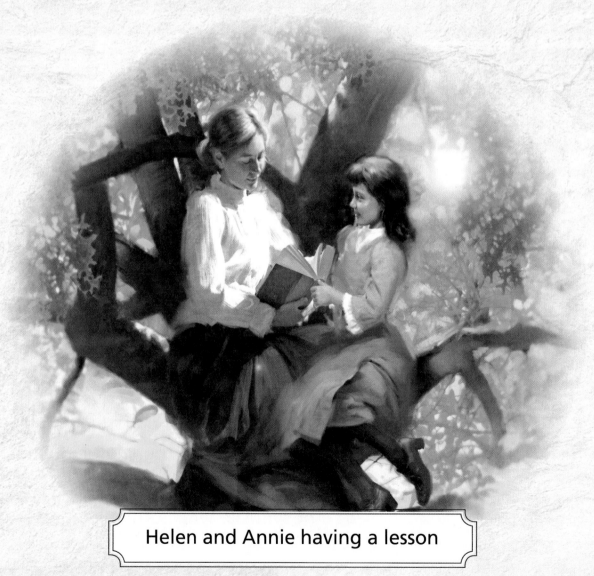

Helen and Annie having a lesson

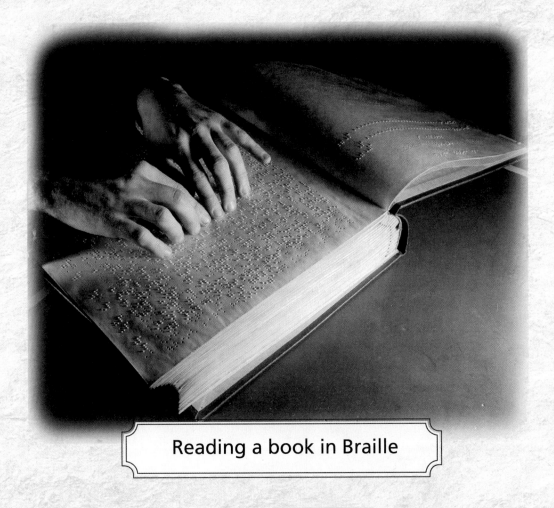

Reading a book in Braille

Helen was hungry for knowledge. She wanted to learn everything Annie could teach her. Soon Annie started teaching Helen how to read. The words were printed in raised letters for a blind person.

Helen felt the words with her fingers. She liked to hunt for words she knew. When she learned to read better, she read her books over and over. Her curious fingers wore down the raised letters.

**STOP AND THINK**
**Author's Craft** What does "hungry" mean in the first sentence?

Helen also learned to write. She wrote letters to her family and Dr. Bell. She wrote many letters to Mr. Anagnos in Boston. Mr. Anagnos was amazed by how much Helen had learned. He published some of Helen's letters. Reporters began to write about Helen. Soon she was famous. People all over the world wanted to know about the miracle girl. And Helen wanted to know all about the world.

# Your Turn

## Choose a Hero

### Take a Vote

Who was a bigger hero, Helen or her teacher? Have your class vote. Then form a small group with others who share your view. List reasons for your choice. Share your ideas with the class. SMALL GROUP

**Who was a bigger hero?**

| Helen | Annie |
|-------|-------|
| ||||| | ||||| |

## Turn and Talk — Big Ideas

Choose a page from the selection. Work with a partner to find the most important idea on that page. Talk about why you think that idea is the most important.

MAIN IDEAS AND DETAILS

Connect to

# Science

✔ TARGET VOCABULARY

| | |
|---|---|
| knowledge | illness |
| curious | imitated |
| motion | darkness |
| silence | behavior |

**GENRE**

**Informational text** gives facts about a topic. This is a science text.

**TEXT FOCUS**

**Photographs** show true pictures of important details. **Captions** tell more information about the photo.

# Talking TOOLS

Helen Keller lived in darkness, but she was curious about the world. Braille helped Keller gain knowledge. Today people who cannot see still use Braille to help them read.

Many ATMs (Automated Teller Machines) have Braille labels, for example. That way, blind people can use them to do their banking.

Some ATMs even talk! With just one quick motion, users plug headphones into the ATM. Then the ATM tells them what to do.

A Braille notetaker is a computer that helps people who cannot see. They type their notes on it, using a Braille keyboard. The notes are saved in Braille. Later they can use their fingers to read the notes in silence on the notepad. The machine can also read the notes aloud!

This girl is using a Braille notetaker. It uses an imitated human voice to read aloud.

speaker

notepad

dot keys

What if someone who cannot see has an illness and needs to take a temperature? Use a talking thermometer! There are talking clocks and watches as well. These watches often have Braille faces, too.

If Helen Keller were alive today, she'd be happy to learn of the many ways technology can help people with vision disabilities.

**Some phones have large numbers and Braille labels. Otherwise, their behavior is just like that of any other phone.**

**Braille labels**

**Button to increase volume**

# Making Connections

 **Text to Self**

**Discuss Learning** Think of some things that Annie taught Helen. Talk with a group about the way you learned these same lessons and how that is different from the way Helen learned. Take turns listening and speaking about the topic.

 **Text to Text**

**Connect to Technology** Which of the tools from "Talking Tools" do you think Helen would have liked to use the most? Share your ideas with a partner.

 **Text to World**

**Write a Paragraph** Think about the Braille equipment that you read about in "Talking Tools." Write a paragraph about ways your town can help blind community members.

# Grammar

**Using Proper Nouns** Names for **days** of the week and **months** begin with capital letters. Each important word in the name of a **holiday** begins with a capital letter, too.

**Academic Language**

days

months

holiday

| Days | Months | Holidays |
|------|--------|----------|
| Monday | March | New Year's Day |
| Friday | July | Thanksgiving Day |
| Saturday | September | Fourth of July |

**Try This!**  **Write each sentence correctly.**

1. Is labor day in september?

2. valentine's day is in february.

3. This monday is earth day.

4. I gave my mother flowers on mother's day.

**Ideas** In your writing, use days, holidays, and dates to tell your reader more about when things happen. Remember to begin the names of days, months, and holidays with a capital letter.

| Without Words That Tell When | With Words That Tell When |
|---|---|
| I read books to a neighbor. She lost her sight. | Every Sunday I read books to a neighbor. She lost her sight on May 25, 2007. |

## Connect Grammar to Writing

**As you revise your persuasive essay next week, think about ways to tell your reader more. Add words that tell when.**

# Write to Persuade

☑ **Ideas** When you write to persuade, give your readers reasons to support your goal.

Farah made a web to plan her **persuasive essay**. She had two reasons. Later, she added details and facts to make her reasons stronger.

## Writing Process Checklist

▶ **Prewrite**

☑ **Did I choose a goal I care about?**

☑ **Did I give reasons that support my goal?**

☑ **Did I include details and facts to make my reasons convincing to my audience?**

**Draft**

**Revise**

**Edit**

**Publish and Share**

**Exploring a Topic**

Goal: Raise Money for Braille Books

Library needs more Braille books

We can help

```
            Goal: Raise Money
             for Braille Books


   Library needs              We can help
   more Braille books


Many        Library      Our         We can
people      has only     school      do a
in town     20           wants a     Read-
read        Braille      community   a-thon
Braille     books        project
```

> I added supporting details to make my reasons more convincing.

## Reading as a Writer

**What details did Farah add? What details can you add to make your reasons more persuasive?**

441

TARGET VOCABULARY

**obeys**

**safety**

**attention**

**buddy**

**station**

**speech**

**shocked**

**enormous**

| Vocabulary Reader | Context Cards |
|---|---|

# Vocabulary in Context

● Read each **Context Card**.

● Tell a story about two pictures, using the Vocabulary words.

### 1 obeys

A careful driver always obeys traffic rules. This driver stops at a stop sign.

### 2 safety

The firefighter talks about fire safety. He teaches about staying out of danger.

### 3 attention

Look both ways and pay attention to traffic before crossing the street.

### 4 buddy

Never swim alone. Always swim with a buddy, or friend.

### 5 station

A police station is a safe place to go if you need help.

### 6 speech

His job is to give a short speech. He will talk about airplane safety.

### 7 shocked

She is shocked at how hot it is outside. She needs to get out of the sun soon!

### 8 enormous

Only the workers can go inside the fence on this enormous work site.

# Background

**Police Officers** Whether they work in an enormous city or a small town, police officers do an important job. They make sure everyone obeys the law. Some officers work at a police station. Others go on patrol with a buddy. Officers may visit a school to give a speech. You should pay attention to their safety tips. Officers are not shocked by questions they get asked. They have seen many things on the job!

This is a map of a police station.

| Locker Room | Storage Room |
| --- | --- |
| Meeting Room | Interview Room |

Front Desk

Waiting Area

Main Entrance

Parking lot for police vehicles

# Comprehension

✔ **TARGET SKILL** **Cause and Effect**

In *Officer Buckle and Gloria*, some events make other things happen. The first event is the cause. The event that is the result of a cause is its effect. Show how the events connect to each other on a chart like this one.

| Cause | Effect |
|-------|--------|
|       |        |

✔ **TARGET STRATEGY** **Monitor/Clarify**

When you read, monitor your understanding of story events. If you don't understand why something is happening, stop and think. Looking for causes and effects can help you understand the story better.

**MEET THE AUTHOR AND ILLUSTRATOR**

# PEGGY RATHMANN

Peggy Rathmann's family had a dog named Skippy. One holiday they were gathered for breakfast. A family member was filming them. It wasn't until later when they were watching the home movie that they caught Skippy in the background, licking the poached eggs on the serving table. No one had seen it happen. Skippy was the model for the dog in *Officer Buckle and Gloria*.

# OFFICER BUCKLE
## AND
# GLORIA

### written and illustrated by
## PEGGY RATHMANN

## Essential Question

What might cause a story character to change?

Officer Buckle knew more safety tips than anyone else in Napville.

Every time he thought of a new one, he thumbtacked it to his bulletin board.

Safety Tip #77
NEVER stand on a SWIVEL CHAIR.

Officer Buckle shared his safety tips with the students at Napville School.

Nobody ever listened.

Sometimes, there was snoring.

Afterward, it was business as usual.

Mrs. Toppel, the principal, took down the welcome banner.

"NEVER stand on a SWIVEL CHAIR," said Officer Buckle, but Mrs. Toppel didn't hear him.

Then one day, Napville's police department bought a police dog named Gloria.

When it was time for Officer Buckle to give the safety speech at the school, Gloria went along.

"Children, this is Gloria," announced Officer Buckle. "Gloria obeys my commands. Gloria, SIT!" And Gloria sat.

Officer Buckle gave Safety Tip Number One:
"KEEP your SHOELACES tied!"
The children sat up and stared.

Officer Buckle checked to see if Gloria was
sitting at attention.  She was.

"Safety Tip Number Two," said Officer Buckle.
"ALWAYS wipe up spills BEFORE someone SLIPS
AND FALLS!"

The children's eyes popped.

Officer Buckle checked on Gloria again.

"Good dog," he said.

Officer Buckle thought of a safety tip he had
discovered that morning.

"NEVER leave a THUMBTACK where you
might SIT on it!"
The audience roared.

Officer Buckle grinned. He said the rest of
the tips with *plenty of* expression.

The children clapped their hands and
cheered. Some of them laughed until they cried.

Officer Buckle was surprised. He had never
noticed how funny safety tips could be.

After *this* safety speech, there wasn't a
single accident.

> ✔️ **STOP AND THINK**
> **Cause and Effect** What
> do the children do when
> Gloria acts out Officer
> Buckle's safety tips?

The next day, an enormous envelope arrived
at the police station.  It was stuffed with thank-you
letters from the students at Napville School.

Every letter had a drawing of Gloria on it.

Officer Buckle thought the drawings showed a
lot of imagination.

**STOP AND THINK**
**Monitor/Clarify**  Why does Officer
Buckle think the students' drawings
show a lot of imagination?

His favorite letter was written on a star-shaped piece of paper. It said:

You and Gloria make a good team.

Your friend,
Claire

P.S. I always wear a crash helmet. (Safety Tip #7)

Officer Buckle was thumbtacking Claire's letter to his bulletin board when the phones started ringing. Grade schools, high schools, and day-care centers were calling about the safety speech.

"Officer Buckle," they said, "our students want to hear your safety tips! And please, bring along that police dog."

457

Officer Buckle told his safety tips to 313 schools.
Everywhere he and Gloria went, children sat up
and listened.

After every speech, Officer Buckle took Gloria out for ice cream.

Officer Buckle loved having a buddy.

Then one day, a television news team videotaped Officer Buckle in the state-college auditorium.

When he finished Safety Tip Number Ninety-nine, DO NOT GO SWIMMING DURING ELECTRICAL STORMS!, the students jumped to their feet and applauded.

"Bravo! Bravo!" they cheered. Officer Buckle bowed again and again.

**STOP AND THINK**
**Author's Craft** The author uses capital letters for some words. Why?

That night, Officer Buckle watched himself
on the 10 o'clock news.

The next day, the principal of Napville School
telephoned the police station.

"Good morning, Officer Buckle! It's time for
our safety speech!"

Officer Buckle frowned.

"I'm not giving any more speeches! Nobody
looks at me, anyway!"

"Oh," said Mrs. Toppel. "Well! How about
Gloria? Could she come?"

Someone else from the police station gave Gloria a ride to the school.

Gloria sat onstage looking lonely. Then she fell asleep. So did the audience.

After Gloria left, Napville School had its biggest accident ever . . .

It started with a puddle of banana pudding. . . .
SPLAT!  SPLATTER! SPLOOSH!

Everyone slid smack into Mrs. Toppel, who screamed
and let go of her hammer.

465

The next morning, a pile of letters arrived at the police station.

Every letter had a drawing of the accident.

Officer Buckle was shocked.

At the bottom of the pile was a note written on a paper star.

Officer Buckle smiled. The note said:

Gloria gave Officer Buckle a big kiss on the nose.

Officer Buckle gave Gloria a nice pat on the back.

Then, Officer Buckle thought of his best safety tip yet . . .

Safety Tip #101

"ALWAYS STICK WITH YOUR BUDDY!"

## Your Turn

### Safe at School

**Write a Tip**

Think of a new tip about school safety. Your tip may be serious or silly. Write your tip on a piece of paper and draw a picture to go with it. Then write a few sentences telling what would happen if people didn't follow your safety tip. Share your tip with classmates. CAUSE AND EFFECT

Turn and Talk ── **Tell About Changes**

Work with a partner. Tell your partner one way that Officer Buckle changed in the story. Have your partner tell what caused the change to happen. Then switch roles. Give another example. CAUSE AND EFFECT

# Social Studies

Safety at Home

✔ **TARGET VOCABULARY**

| | |
|---|---|
| obeys | station |
| safety | speech |
| attention | shocked |
| buddy | enormous |

**GENRE**

**Readers' Theater** is a text that has been written for readers to read aloud.

**TEXT FOCUS**

**Directions** tell how to do something step-by-step. As you read, pay attention to how dialogue is used to give directions.

# Safety at Home

**by Margaret Sweeny**

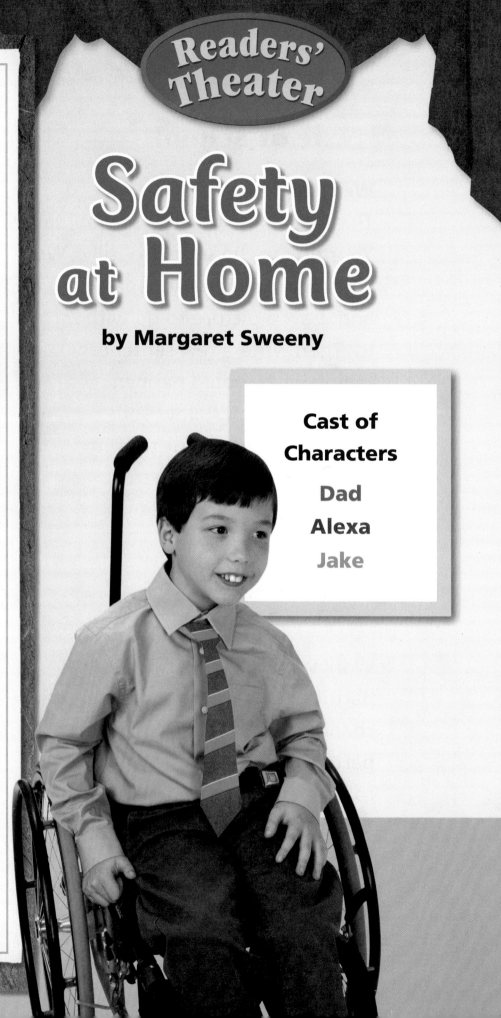

**Cast of Characters**

Dad

Alexa

Jake

**Dad:** What did you do on your class trip?

**Alexa:** We visited an enormous fire station.

**Jake:** The fire chief gave a speech about fire safety.

**Dad:** I hope you were paying attention.

**Alexa:** We were. Later, we worked with a buddy to make a safety poster. I worked with Jake.

**Jake:** Look at our poster.

STOP, DROP, AND ROLL

1. If your clothes catch on fire, don't run.

2. STOP where you are.

3. DROP to the ground. Cover your face with your hands.

4. ROLL over and over to put out the fire.

**Dad:** I'm shocked! You know more about fire safety than I do.

**Alexa:** Everyone in our school obeys fire safety rules.

**Jake:** Guess what **get low and go** means?

**Alexa:** If the house is smoky, get low.

**Jake:** That's because smoke rises. Get low to stay below the smoke.

**Alexa:** Crawl to the nearest way out.

**Jake:** Then go to a safe meeting place to wait for your family.

**Dad:** Let's pick a meeting place right now!

# Making Connections

 **Text to Self**

**Write a Caption** Officer Buckle's safety tips are based on his own life. Think of a safety tip you learned. Draw a picture of what Gloria might do to act out that tip. Then write a caption for your picture.

 **Text to Text**

**Compare and Contrast** How are Officer Buckle's safety tips like the tips from *Safety at Home*? How are they different? Talk about it with a partner.

 **Text to World**

**Connect to Social Studies** Gloria acted out safety tips, and Alexa and Jake made a fire safety poster. Think about some classroom safety tips. Make a poster for your classroom.

# Grammar

**Abbreviations** The names of days, months, and places are proper nouns that can be shortened. An **abbreviation** is a short way to write a word by taking out some of the letters and writing a period at the end.

**Academic Language**

abbreviation

| Proper Nouns | Abbreviations |
|---|---|
| Monday | Mon. |
| March | Mar. |
| Main Street | Main St. |

 **Write the proper noun for each abbreviation.**

❶ Nov.        ❹ Canton St.

❷ Tues.       ❺ Jan.

❸ Elm Rd.     ❻ Fri.

474

**Conventions** In your writing, make sure you write abbreviations correctly. Remember to use a period at the end of an abbreviation.

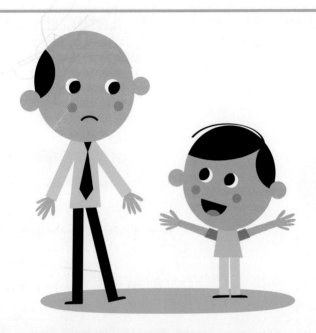

| Incorrect | Correct |
|---|---|
| mr Wang says the police officer will visit our class on sept 4. | Mr. Wang says the police officer will visit our class on Sept. 4. |

## Connect Grammar to Writing

**When you edit your persuasive essay, make sure you have used capital letters and end marks correctly.**

# Write to Persuade

☑ **Organization** When you write a **persuasive essay**, each reason can start a new paragraph.

Farah wrote a draft of her essay. Later, she moved things around so each reason started a new paragraph.

## Writing Process Checklist

**Prewrite**

**Draft**

▶ **Revise**

☑ Did I tell my goal in a clear way?

☑ Did I give reasons for my goal?

☑ Did I include facts and examples for each reason?

☑ Did I sum up my reasons?

**Edit**

**Publish and Share**

### Revised Draft

Our town library has a problem. ¶There are thirty-four people in our town who read Braille. The library has only twenty Braille It needs more. books. It needs money for Braille books. ¶Our school wants to do a community project. Helping the library would be a good one for us.

# Help Our Library!

by Farah Jamali

Our town library has a problem. It needs money for Braille books.

There are thirty-four people in our town who read Braille. The library has only twenty Braille books. It needs more.

Our school is looking for a community project. Helping the library would be a good one for us. We could have a Read-a-thon to raise money for Braille books. Each student can fill out a pledge sheet.

I started a new paragraph for each reason.

## Reading as a Writer

How did Farah organize her essay to make her reasons clearer? How can you organize your reasons and details?

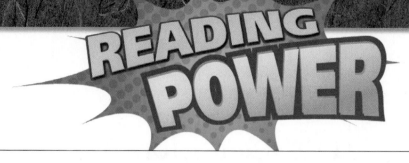

# A Furry Best Friend

The yellow dog named Toby stays close to Jenna. When Jenna walks, Toby walks with her. Toby is special. His job is to take care of Jenna.

Jenna does not see well. Toby went to a special dog school where he learned to see for Jenna. He leads Jenna around things that may be in her way.

Toby guides Jenna across a street. He looks both ways for cars. He makes sure it is safe for Jenna to cross.

"Good job, Toby!" says Jenna. She and Toby are a team.

# Willie the Hero

In March 2009, a parrot named Willie won the Animal Lifesaver Award. Willie was the first bird to win. The award usually goes to hero dogs.

Willie lives with his owner and her little girl. He can speak a few words. Mostly, Willie speaks when he wants food.

One day Willie was alone with the little girl. The babysitter went into another room for a few seconds. The girl choked on a piece of food. Willie began to yell, "Momma, Baby! Momma, Baby!"

The babysitter ran back into the room. She helped the girl. She said that Willie was a hero. He saved the girl's life.

# Unit 3 Wrap-Up

## The Big Idea

**We Learn from Each Other**
Make a book to share with a younger child. Your book should tell how to do or make something. Draw pictures and write words on each page. What will this younger child learn from your book?

## Listening and Speaking

**Look What I Can Do** Think of something that you know how to do well, such as making a paper airplane. Teach the class how to do that thing. Use your best speaking voice as you teach.

# Glossary

This glossary can help you find the meanings of some of the words in this book. The meanings given are the meanings of the words as they are used in the book. Sometimes a second meaning is also given.

## A

**alone**

Without anyone or anything: *Sometimes she liked to be alone in the tree house and read stories.*

**attend**

To look carefully at or take care of: *We try to attend to the work we are asked to do.*

**attention**

A form of **attend**: *When someone read a story to them, their attention was very good.*

## B

**beak**

A bill, or the hard mouth parts of a bird: *The baby birds opened their beaks wide, waiting for their food.*

**behave**

To act in a certain way: *We always tried to behave well when visitors were in the room.*

**behavior**

A form of **behave**: *His behavior in school was better than it was at home.*

**believe**

To accept as true or real: *I believe that you have the hat.*

**bend**

To become curved or not straight: *The tree branches bend down in the heavy snow.*

**beak**

## beware

To be careful or look out for a problem: *The sign told us to* **beware** *of falling rocks.*

## bloom

To blossom or grow into flower: *Some plants* **bloom** *in the spring, while others are just starting to grow.*

**bloom**

## blooming

A form of **bloom**: *Butterflies come to the garden when that bush is* **blooming**.

## brag

To boast, or speak with too much pride: *She tries not to* **brag** *about winning, but she wants us to know.*

## branch

A part that grows out from a trunk of a tree: *All the* **branches** *of the tree had yellow leaves.*

## break

To separate into pieces or tear apart: *We had to* **break** *the ground up with different garden tools.*

## breeze

A light wind: *The puppy smelled smoke when she sniffed the* **breeze**.

## buddy

A pal or close friend: *He became my* **buddy** *during our first summer in camp.*

## burst

To be full to the point of breaking open: *She tried hard not to* **burst** *out laughing when she saw the silly hat.*

## bursting

A form of **burst**: *The milkweed pod was **bursting** with silky seeds.*

bursting

## busy

To be actively at work: *The **busy** squirrel gathered nuts.*

# C

## chipmunk

An animal that looks similar to a squirrel but is smaller and has a striped back: *Three brown **chipmunks** chased each other up the tree in our backyard.*

## choice

The act of choosing or the chance to choose: *We had many **choices** about what to see in the city.*

## collar

A leather, cloth, or metal band for an animal's neck: *Both of our dogs wear red **collars** around their necks.*

## community

A group of people who live together in the same area: *Our **community** is filled with friendly neighbors.*

## cousin

A child of one's aunt or uncle: *My **cousin** stayed with us for two days.*

## crown

A head covering that a queen, king, or other ruler might wear: *She used paper, glue, and glitter to make a **crown** for her costume.*

**crown**

## culture

The traditions, arts, and beliefs of a certain group of people: *In his Native American **culture**, the fall harvest is a time for celebration.*

## curious

Eager to find out or learn about something: *He was **curious** about many kinds of sea animals, so he loved the aquarium.*

## curl

To make a rounded shape: *He showed us how to **curl** slices of carrot in cold water.*

## curled

A form of **curl**: *The kitten **curled** up in his lap and purred happily.*

## curly

A form of **curl**: *My brother's hair is so thick and **curly** he can hardly comb it.*

# D

## damage

To harm or injure: *The flood might **damage** the bridge so that it must be closed for repair.*

## danger

The chance of harm, or something that may cause harm: *We had good reasons to worry about **danger** deep in the dark cave.*

## dangerous

A form of **danger**: *The little rabbit knew it was a **dangerous** place, but she hopped closer.*

**dark**

Without light or with very little light: *With no moon, the night was **dark**.*

**darkness**

A form of **dark**: *In the **darkness**, he couldn't tell what kind of animal was outside.*

**decide**

To make up one's mind: *Tomorrow I will **decide** what to do about the party.*

**deep**

Located far below the surface or far from an opening: *They buried the treasure **deep** in the ground near a pine tree.*

**deepest**

A form of **deep**: *In the **deepest** part of the ocean, it is very dark.*

**demand**

To ask firmly or to require: *The teachers in that school **demand** hard work from their students.*

**direction**

The place or line along which someone or something goes: *Walk in the **direction** of the town.*

direction

**disgust**

To cause a sick or bad feeling: *If those movies **disgust** you, please stop watching them.*

**disgusting**

A form of **disgust**: *When she sniffed at the garbage pail, it smelled **disgusting**.*

**drift**

To float along or be carried along on water or air: *Our raft will **drift** if we do not paddle.*

**drool**

To let saliva drip from the mouth: *My baby sister **drools** on my arm and makes my sleeve wet.*

**drooled**

A form of **drool**: *He **drooled** when he looked at all the delicious food.*

# E

**enormous**

Huge, or very large in size: *Hank was an **enormous** dog, almost the size of a cow.*

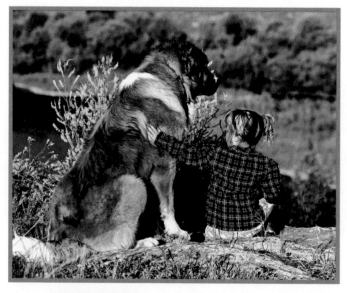

**enormous**

**equal**

To be the same as: *Seven days **equal** one week, and twenty-four hours equal one day.*

# F

**flash**

To give out a sudden bright light: *The fireworks **flash** in the night sky, and people cheer.*

**flash**

**flop**

To drop or hang heavily: *When I'm really tired, I **flop** onto the couch for a nap.*

**floppy**

A form of flop: *Some rabbits have **floppy** ears that droop around their face.*

**furious**

Full of great anger, or raging: *She was so **furious** that she threw a pillow across the room.*

# G

**gather**

To bring or come together in one place: *We will **gather** for the meeting at noon today.*

**gathered**

A form of **gather**: *After the whole group **gathered** on stage, they began to sing.*

**grew**

A form of grow: *My dad **grew** a big, thick beard that almost covered his face!*

**grow**

To get bigger, increase, or spread: *That little patch of flowers is starting to **grow** across the whole yard.*

# H

**hang**

To be attached at the upper end: *Many colorful paintings **hang** on the walls of the museum.*

**heal**

To get better or become well: *Most cuts **heal** quickly if you take care of them.*

**healed**

A form of **heal**: *When the deer's leg **healed**, she ran as fast as ever.*

**height**

The distance from bottom to top: *The **height** of the mountain is about a mile above sea level.*

**height**

G7

## hour

A unit of time that equals sixty minutes: *They spent many hours playing games at camp.*

# I

## ill

Sick or not healthy: *They have been ill with the flu.*

## illness

A form of **ill**: *After an illness, people may feel tired for a few days.*

## imitate

To copy the actions, looks, or sounds of: *Little children imitate their parents or older children in their family.*

## imitated

A form of **imitate**: *After I imitated the steps many times, I learned to do the dance.*

## impatient

Not able or willing to wait: *She walked because she was too impatient to wait for the bus.*

## impossible

Not possible or not able to happen: *It will be impossible to finish on time unless you start now.*

## inform

To tell about something: *The guide informs people about animals on the nature trail.*

## insect

A bug that has six legs, a body with three main parts, and, usually, wings: *She liked to watch insects at the pond.*

insect

# J

## judge

To listen or look at in order to decide about: *At the fair, it was fun to **judge** which pie should win the first prize.*

# K

## know

To understand or have the facts about: *Do you **know** what causes thunder?*

## knowledge

Facts and ideas, or information: *Their teacher had **knowledge** about many subjects, such as weather and history.*

# L

## language

A system of words, expressions, signs, or symbols shared by a group of people: *At our house we speak two **languages**: Spanish and English.*

## lesson

Something to be learned or taught: *After a few more **lessons**, I'll be able to skate like an Olympic athlete!*

# M

## millions

A very large number, or more than a thousand thousands: *There are **millions** of fish in the sea.*

## motion

Movement, gesture, or the act of moving: *The **motion** of the boat on the waves made him feel sleepy.*

## muscle

Body tissue that helps many different parts of the body move and work: *Our **muscles** will get stronger from all the exercise we do.*

### museum

A building where art or other important things are displayed, or shown: *The **museum** he liked best had many buttons to press and things to do.*

# N

### nod

To move the head down and up in a quick motion that may mean "okay": *You will be out of the game if you move before I **nod** my head.*

### nodded

A form of **nod**: *I was glad when my father **nodded** to let us know we could go.*

### noise

A sound that may be loud or unpleasant: *You could tell from the **noises** that there were many animals in the barn.*

### notice

To pay attention to or make note of: *I sat in the back and hoped that nobody would **notice** me.*

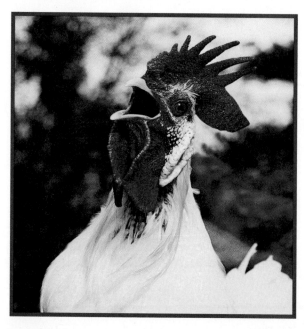

noise

### noticed

A form of **notice**: *The first thing he **noticed** was how fast the clouds moved across the sky.*

### nursery

A room for babies or young children: *He remembered playing happily in the **nursery**.*

# O

### obey

To do what is asked: *After training, the horse **obeys** the rider.*

# P

## piano

A musical instrument with a keyboard: *She could play tunes on the piano.*

**piano**

## pick

Gather: *If you pick some wildflowers, I'll put them in a vase for Aunt Mimi.*

## picked

A form of **pick**: *We picked enough berries from our garden to make twelve pies!*

## plain

Not fancy or pretty: *The plants look plain before they bloom.*

## pond

A small body of water in the shape of a lake or pool: *Frogs sat at the edge of the pond.*

## porch

A structure with a roof that is attached to the outside of a house: *They kept two chairs and a low table on the porch.*

## pound

To hammer or hit hard again and again: *When you pound on the drum, I want to leave the room.*

## pounding

A form of **pound**: *The pounding rain on the tent kept her from falling asleep.*

## prevent

To stop or keep from happening: *You can prevent fires by being careful.*

### problem

Something that is difficult to deal with or understand: *The group tried to solve the* **problem** *by talking together.*

# Q

### quiet

Silent, calm, or with hardly any sound: *The house was finally* **quiet** *after all the children were asleep.*

# R

### reach

To get to or go as far as: *When all the boats* **reach** *the shore, I will feel better.*

### real

Not imagined or made up: *She wanted to have a* **real** *pet and not just a toy animal.*

### remember

To think of again or bring back in the mind: *I* **remember** *the first word I learned to read.*

### remembered

A form of **remember**: *He always* **remembered** *his grandpa's stories.*

### rotten

Decayed or spoiled: *Some insects eat* **rotten** *fruit that people throw away.*

### row

In a line or in sequence, one after another: *I got an A on two tests in a* **row**, *which is a new record for me!*

# S

### safe

Free from danger or harm: *The mother bird saw that her babies were* **safe** *in the nest.*

**safe**

**safety**

A form of **safe**: *Most playground rules were made for your* ***safety***.

**scare**

To frighten or make afraid: *This dragon mask might* ***scare*** *some little children.*

**scent**

A special smell that comes from something: *The* ***scent*** *of roses reminded her of her grandmother's yard in the spring.*

scent

**scream**

To make a long, loud, high-pitched cry: *When my little sister* ***screams***, *I hold my ears.*

**screaming**

A form of **scream**: *When the game got close, many people started* ***screaming*** *for their team to win.*

**shake**

To move quickly up and down or back and forth: *He sometimes will* ***shake*** *the toy bank to hear the coins inside.*

**shape**

To give a certain form or shape to: *I* ***shape*** *the clay to look like woodland animals.*

**shaped**

A form of **shape**: *The sign at the farm stand was large and* ***shaped*** *like a pumpkin.*

**share**

To divide with others or take part in: *Let's* ***share*** *this last orange.*

### shock

To surprise or greatly upset: *The news will **shock** you, so please sit down.*

### shocked

A form of **shock**: *I was **shocked** when I found that the jewels were missing.*

### shovel

A tool with a long handle and a flattened scoop: *The man is using a snow **shovel**.*

**shovel**

### silence

A form of **silent**: *The **silence** in the library helps people enjoy their reading.*

### silent

Quiet, making or having no sound: *The room was **silent**, so she thought everyone had gone.*

### simple

Easy, or not complicated: *The directions on the box looked **simple**, and she followed them carefully.*

### smooth

Going along evenly, or without rough parts: *The custard was **smooth** and made her sore throat feel better.*

### south

The direction to the left of a person who faces the sunset: *My grandparents go **south** each winter to bask in the warm weather.*

**special**

Different from what is common or usual: *Birthdays are* **special** *occasions.*

**speech**

The act of speaking, or a talk: *She practiced at home before she gave the* **speech** *in class.*

**spend**

To cause or allow time to pass: *We will* **spend** *the day at the beach.*

**sprinkle**

To scatter in drops or small pieces: *We always* **sprinkle** *salt into the water before it boils.*

**sprinkled**

A form of **sprinkle**: *The children* **sprinkled** *fish food into the goldfish bowl.*

**stand**

To be a certain height: *Medium-size dogs usually* **stand** *between two and three feet tall.*

**station**

A place where a special service is provided: *We got our tickets and waited at the train* **station**.

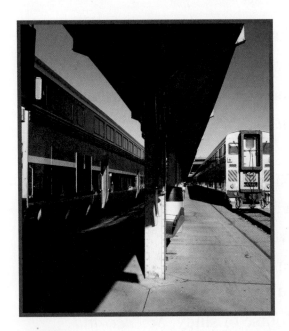

station

**stick**

To attach or to keep in one place: *We* **stick** *a stamp on each card before we mail it.*

**sticky**

Holding together as with glue or hard to pull apart: *After eating the honey, they licked their* **sticky** *fingers.*

**stood**

A form of **stand**: *Last year my sister **stood** three feet tall, but now she's almost four feet.*

**straight**

Not curving, curling, or bending: *My hair is **straight** and never gets wavy.*

**stuck**

A form of **stick**: *The truck got **stuck** in the heavy snow.*

**subject**

Course of study: *Science and social studies are his favorite **subjects** in school.*

**sudden**

Happening or coming without warning: *On the hike, we were caught in a **sudden** storm.*

**suddenly**

A form of **sudden**: *The birds flew away as **suddenly** as they had landed in the yard.*

# T

**tease**

To make fun of or try to bother: *My friends used to **tease** me about my hair.*

**top**

The highest or upper part: *The **tops** of those mountains are covered in snow.*

**tough**

Strong and not likely to break or wear out: *The hiking boots were warm and **tough,** so he could walk outdoors in any weather.*

**toward**

In the direction of: *We walked **toward** the tower and watched for a light.*

**transportation**

Means of getting from one place to another: *Trains are my favorite kind of **transportation**.*

## tunnel

A passage underground or underwater: *The train passed through the* **tunnel** *to the other side of the mountain.*

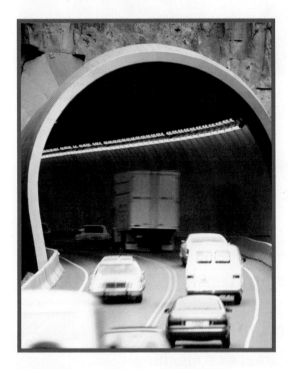

**tunnel**

## turn

Transform; change: *When the skies* **turn** *from blue to gray, a storm is on the way.*

## turned

A form of **turn**: *The weather* **turned** *colder as soon as the calendar said fall.*

# U

## understand

To get the meaning of: *I* **understand** *the meaning of a few Spanish words.*

# V

## visit

To go or come to see: *We will* **visit** *our friends in the city.*

# W

## weak

Having little or no power, strength, or energy: *The battery was so* **weak** *that our flashlight didn't help much.*

## weaker

A form of **weak**: *She was* **weaker** *after being sick, but then she grew stronger.*

## wear

To have on the body: *In cold places, people* **wear** *two or three layers of clothes.*

### weigh

Find out the weight or heaviness of: *The doctor will* **weigh** *you on a scale before your checkup.*

### weighed

A form of weigh: *I* **weighed** *my dog three times to make sure she was really that heavy!*

### whenever

At whatever time: **Whenever** *it rains, my cat wants to come inside.*

### wind

To move along with twists and turns: *We* **wind** *the string around the stick to bring the kite back in.*

### winding

A form of **wind**: *They followed a* **winding** *path higher and higher up the mountain.*

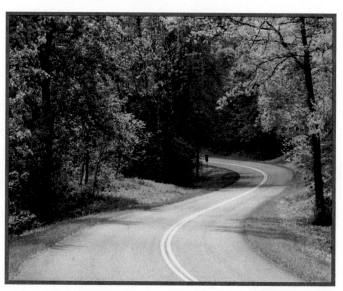

winding

### wonder

A marvel or something amazing: *Their tricks on the high wire were a* **wonder** *to everyone who watched.*

### wonderful

A form of **wonder**: *Their day at the beach was* **wonderful** *from beginning to end.*

## woods

Forest: *Rashid walked quietly through the **woods**, looking for birds in the trees.*

## wrap

To cover by winding or folding: ***Wrap** a scarf around your neck before you go out in the cold wind.*

## wrapped

A form of **wrap**: *We **wrapped** our sandwiches in foil for the picnic.*

**wrapped**

## wrinkle

To form small, uneven lines or creases: *This cloth will **wrinkle** after you wash it, so you need an iron.*

## wrinkled

A form of **wrinkle**: *The shirt was **wrinkled**, so she tried to smooth it out.*

G20

# Acknowledgments

## Main Literature Selections

"Abuelita's Lap" from *Confetti: Poems for Children*, by Pat Mora. Text copyright © 1996 by Pat Mora. Reprinted by permission of Lee & Low Books, Inc.

*Animals Building Homes* by Wendy Perkins. Copyright © 2004 by Capstone Press. All rights reserved. Reprinted by permission of Capstone Press Publishers.

"The Best" from *Did You See What I Saw?* by Kay Winters. Copyright © 1996 by Kay Winters. Reprinted by permission of Viking Penguin, A Division of Penguin Young Readers Group, A Member of Penguin Group (USA) Inc. All rights reserved.

*Click, Clack, Moo: Cows That Type* by Doreen Cronin, illustrated by Betsy Lewin. Text copyright © 2000 by Doreen Cronin. Illustrations copyright © 2000 by Betsy Lewin. Reprinted by permission of Simon & Schuster's Books for Young Readers, an Imprint of Simon & Schuster's Children's Publishing Division. All rights reserved.

*Diary of a Spider* by Doreen Cronin, illustrated by Harry Bliss. Text copyright © 2005 by Doreen Cronin. Illustrations copyright © 2005 by Harry Bliss. Reprinted by permission of HarperCollins Children's Books, a division of HarperCollins Publishers, and Pippin Properties, Inc.

"Everybody Says" from *Everything and Anything* by Dorothy Aldis, copyright © 1925-1927, renewed 1953-1955 by Dorothy Aldis. Reprinted by permission of G.P. Putnam's Sons, A Division of Penguin Young Readers Group, A Member of Penguin Group (USA) Inc. All rights reserved.

*Henry and Mudge: The First Book* by Cynthia Rylant, illustrated by Suçie Stevenson. Text copyright © 1987 by Cynthia Rylant. Illustrations copyright © 1997 by Suçie Stevenson. Reprinted by permission of Simon & Schuster's Books for Young Readers, an imprint of Simon & Schuster Children's Publishing Division. All rights reserved.

*Henry and Mudge Under the Yellow Moon* by Cynthia Rylant, illustrated by Suçie Stevenson. Text copyright © 1987 by Cynthia Rylant. Illustrations copyright © 1997 by Suçie Stevenson. Reprinted by permission of Simon & Schuster Children's Publishing Division. All rights reserved.

*How Chipmunk Got His Stripes* by Joseph and James Bruchac, illustrated by José Aruego & Ariane Dewey. Text copyright © 2001 by Joseph Bruchac and James Bruchac. Illustrations copyright © 2001 by José Aruego and Ariane Dewey. All rights reserved. Published by permission of Dial Books for Young Readers, a member of Penguin Books for Young Readers, a division of Penguin Group (USA) Inc.

"I Have To Write A Poem For Class" from *What A Day It Was At School!* by Jack Prelutsky. Copyright © 2006 by Jack Prelutsky. Reprinted by permission of HarperCollins Publishers.

*Jellies: The Life of Jellyfish* by Twig C. George. Text copyright © 2000 by Twig C. George. All rights reserved. Reprinted by permission of Millbrook Press, a division of Lerner Publishing Group, and Curtis Brown, Ltd.

*Mi Familia/My Family* by George Ancona, children's drawings by Camila Carballo, photographs by George Ancona. Text copyright © 2004 by George Ancona. Children's drawings copyright © 2004 by Camila Carballo. Photographs copyright © 2004 by George Ancona. All rights reserved. Reprinted by permission of Children's Press, an imprint of Scholastic Library Publishing, Inc.

"Morning Sun" from *Laughing Tomatoes and Other Spring Poems* by Francisco X. Alarcón. Copyright © 1997 by Francisco X. Alarcón. Reprinted by permission of the publisher, Children's Book Press, San Francisco, CA, www.childrensbookpress.org.

*Officer Buckle and Gloria* written and illustrated by Peggy Rathmann. Text and illustrations copyright © 1995 by Peggy Rathmann. All rights reserved. Reprinted by permission of G. P. Putnam's Sons, a division of Penguin Putnam Books for Young Readers, a division of Penguin Group (USA) Inc., and Sheldon Fogelman Agency, Inc.

"Rain" by Shisei-Jo from *Japanese Haiku*, translated by Peter Beilenson. Copyright © 1955-56 by Peter Pauper Press. Reprinted by permission of Peter Pauper Press.

"School" from *Hello School!: A Room Full of Poems* by Dee Lillegard, illustrated by Don Carter. Copyright © 2001 by Dee Lillegard. Reprinted by permission of Alfred A. Knopf, an imprint of Random House Children's Books, a division of Random House, Inc., and BookStop Literary Agency, LLC.

*Schools Around the World* by Margaret C. Hall. Originally published as Schools. Text copyright © 2002 Heinemann Library. Reprinted by permission of Heinemann Library, a division of Pearson Education.

*Super Storms* by Seymour Simon. Text copyright © 2002 by Seymour Simon. All rights reserved. Reprinted by permission of Chronicle Books, LLC, San Francisco, California, USA.

*Teacher's Pets* by Dale Ann Dodds, illustrated by Marilyn Hafner. Text copyright © 2006 by Dale Ann Dodds. Illustrations copyright © 2006 by Marilyn Hafner. Reprinted by permission of the publisher, Candlewick Press Inc.

*The Ugly Vegetables* written and illustrated by Grace Lin. Text and illustrations copyright © 1999 by Grace Lin. All rights reserved. Reprinted by permission of Charlesbridge Publishing, Inc.

Excerpt from "What is a family?" from *Fathers, Mothers, Sisters, Brothers: A Collection of Family Poems* by Mary Ann Hoberman. Copyright © 1991 Mary Ann Hoberman. Reprinted by permission of Little Brown & Company and Gina Maccoby Literary Agency.

# Credits

## Photo Credits

**Placement Key:** (t) top; (b) bottom; (l) left; (r) right; (c) center; (bg) background; (fg) foreground; (i) inset.

**8a** Andy Sacks/Getty Images; **8b** Andy Sacks/Getty Images; **9** Andy Sacks/Getty Images; **10** (tl) Arco Images GmbH/Alamy; **10** (tr) (c)Jeffy Shulman/ SuperStock; **11** (tl) Sean MacLeay/Shutterstock; **11** 9tr) (c)Dave Stamboulis/Alamy; **11** (cl) blickwinkel/ Alamy; **11** (cr) (c)Jeff Greenberg/Alamy; **11** (bl) (c)David Burton/Alamy; **11** (br) (c) Manor Photography/alamy; **12** Gandee Vasan/Stone/ Getty Image; **12-13** (c)Blomingimage/Corbis; **14** (t) Courtesy MacMillan; **14** (b) Courtesy Kirchoff Wohlberg; **26** (bkgd) (c)Tony Tayor/San Antonio Zoo; **26** (inset) (c)Don Despain/www. rekindlephotos.com/Alamy; **27** (tl) (c) Scott Doll/ San Antonio Zoo; **27** (cr) Gandee Vasan/Ston/ Getty Images; **27** (br) Photodisc/Getty Images; **28** (inset) (c) GK Hart/Vikki Hart/Riser/Getty Images; **28-29** (bkgd) San Antonio Zoo; **29** (inset) (c)Tim Graham/The Image Bank/Getty Images; **33** HMCo; **34** (t) Edgardo Contreras/Getty Images; **34** (b) Patrick Molnar/Getty Images; **35** (tl) (c) Photodisc/SuperStock; **35** (tr) Alaskastock; **35** (cl) (c) Tom Stewart/CORBIS; **35** (cr) David Young-Wolff/ Photo Edit; **35** (bl) (c) Ronnie Kaufman/Age Fotostock; **35** (br) Masterfile (Royalty-Free Div.); **36** Yellow Dog Productions/ Getty Images; **38-52** Courtesy George Ancona; **54** (c) Stockbyte/Alamy; **54** (tl) Digital Vision/ Alamy; **55** (tr)(c) Jack Hollingsworth/Photodisc/ Getty Images; **56** (b) (c) Digital Vision/Alamy; **57** (t) (c)Stockbyte/SuperStock ; **61** HMCo; **62** (t) (c) Ryan McVay/Getty Images; **62** (b) Digital Vision/ Getty Images; **63** (tl) Photodisc/Getty Images; **63** (tr) (c) Tomakazu Yamada/Getty Images; **63** (cl) (c) Jose Luis Pelaez/Stone/Getty Images; **63** (cr) (c) Anne Ackermann/Taxi/Getty Images; **63** (bl) (c) Rachel Husband/Alamy; **63** (br) (c) Tom Stock/ Stone/Getty Images; **64** (c) blickwinkel/Alamy; **66** (t) Courtesy MacMillan; **66** (b) Courtesy Kirchoff Wohlberg; **78-79** (c) Gary Crabbe/age fotostock; **79** (b) (c) Darrell Gulin/Stone/Getty Images; **80** (bl) (c) Amanda Hall/Getty Images; **80** (br) Photodisc/Getty Images; **80-81** (bkgd) Corel Stock/Photo Library; **85** HMCo; **86** (t) FABIO COLOMBINI MEDEIROS/Animals Animals - Earth Scenes; **86** (b) John B Free/npl/Minden Pictures; **87** (tl) (c) Stephanie Pilick/dpa/Corbis; **87** (tr) Getty Images; **87** (cl) (c) Bilderbuch/ Design Pics/Corbis; **87** (cr) Michael & Patricia Fogden/Minden Pictures; **87** (bl) (c) Tony Arruza/ CORBIS; **87** (br) (c) Buddy Mays/CORBIS; **88** (c) Bartomeu Borrell/age fotostock; **90** (t) Courtesy Harper Collins; **90** (b) Courtesy Harry Bliss; **102** Birgid Allig/Getty Images; **102-103** (c) Getty Images; **104** (c) Getty Images; **121** HMCo; **122** (t) Arthur Tilley/Getty Images; **122** (b) Daniel Dempster Photography/Alamy; **123** (tl) Richard Hutchings/Photo Edit; **123** (tr) Sean Justice/Getty Images; **123** (cl) Juniors Bildarchiv/Alamy; **123** (cr) imagebroker/Alamy; **123** (bl) Bill Losh/Getty Images; **123** (br) Michael Newman/Photo Edit; **124** (c) Paul Hardy/Corbis; **157** HMCo; **162** (t) (c) Joseph Sohm/Visions of America/Corbis; **162** (b) Peter Oxford/Minden Picturers;